Paul Vanderbroeck
Jannie Aasted Skov-Hansen

HERE WE ARE
The International Career Couple Handbook

First published in Great Britain in 2020 by Springtime Books

Text © by Paul Vanderbroeck; Jannie Aasted Skov-Hansen
Illustrations © by Anne Bundgaard

All rights reserved. No part of this publication may be reproduced, stored in or introduced into a retrieval system, or transmitted, in any form, or by any means (electronic, mechanical, photocopying recording or otherwise) without the prior written permission of the publisher.

This book is sold subject to the condition that it shall not, by way of trade or otherwise, be lent, resold, hired out, or otherwise circulated without the publisher's prior consent in any form of binding or cover other than that in which it is published and without a similar condition including this condition being imposed on the subsequent purchaser.

ISBN: 978-1-8381746-0-6

Illustrations and layout designed by:
Anne Bundgaard
www.annebundgaard.dk

BOOK REVIEWS

"If only we had this toolbox earlier as an International Career Couple! It would have made our journey of many years in multiple countries a lot easier. In our professional and social networks, we often met couples who were struggling with the same issues of combining two careers, a family and international mobility. This well-researched, practical and inspiring handbook is a must-read for couples and employers alike!"

Nicholas Brassey Chief HR Officer Ahold Delhaize Europe and Indonesia
Jacqui Brassey, PhD, Director of Learning, Enduring Priorities & Global Learning at McKinsey & Company

"We love that the book coins the term International Career Couple. As an ICC, we have often talked about how we face different challenges than other couples. This book will do for ICCs what Third Culture Kids *has done for our children. Thankfully, the book does not pretend that you can make a fixed plan – the need for regular revisits is in our experience a key message. Also, high sensitivity to each other's needs and worries are essential in order to overcome the compromises needed along the way. This handbook offers a good structure for the deep reflections and discussions you need to have as an ICC."*

Sandra Jensen Landi, Ambassador of Denmark to Singapore and Brunei
Martin Landi, Senior Global Adviser

"The authors offer useful advice, guidelines and exercises for couples who both work abroad in an international/multilateral environment and their employers alike. In my experience there are more and more of such couples. Not all Ministries of Foreign Affairs and multilateral organizations, like the UN and the EU, have yet entirely come to grips with the complexities of dual international career couples in their workforce."

Jean-Pierre Kempeneers, Ambassador for International Positions, Ministry of Foreign Affairs of the Netherlands

"Writing this book was an act of enormous courage. The topic of ICCs is incredibly complex. It requires addressing the intersection of career planning with a person's personal and family life, compounded by dealing with two people versus one. Add to that the dimension of different cultures and languages coming together. The authors provide painstaking analysis and practical solutions derived from extensive research.

In addition to those contemplating working in such an arrangement, this book has value for the HR leaders of global organizations who increasingly employ such couples. The reality, however, is that every couple would find enormous value in the practical, comprehensive recommendations the authors present for planning your life together with another person.

This groundbreaking book is highly recommended to all who are, or who plan to live with someone else in a way that enables both to have a totally fulfilling life."

Jack Zenger, CEO of Zenger Folkman, best-selling author of *The Extraordinary Leader: Turning Great Managers into Great Leaders.*

"This book is a must-read for couples starting or having an international career. It provides both a holistic framework and a lot of practical tools; and describes opportunities and challenges that will be well recognized by International Career Couples. It clearly makes you reflect on how to find the necessary balance in combining a dual career, a family and social life and international mobility."

Helena Vanhoutte,
General Manager France, Vandemoortele

"The International Career Couple Handbook is an invaluable resource for today's mobile couples. Packed full of lively case studies and engaging exercises its a handy guide for couples trying to juggle two international careers and a fulfilling relationship. A must read for all international career couples!"

Jennifer Petriglieri,
Associate Professor INSEAD, Author Couples That Work: How Dual-Career Couples Can Thrive in Love and Work (HBR Press)

"Finally, a book that recognizes the importance and complexity of International Career Couples. In it, the writers provide useful insights and tools for both: career couples and their employers to extract value of their investment in such demanding transitions and maximize their return for both individual growth and organizational performance. A highly recommended read for both international career individuals, their bosses, and Human Resources professionals."

Shlomo Ben-Hur,
Professor of Leadership and Organizational Behavior at IMD.

7

"After 30 years of my own research and that of others, it is clear that international assignments are the most powerful means of developing future global leaders and one of the most powerful forces in shaping individual's lives. Having lived and worked overseas multiple times, I also know this from personal experience. However, international assignments for dual career couples can be both wonderful and challenging. Couples need a grounded but practical guide. HERE WE ARE: The International Career Couple Handbook is just that — the handbook that any and every international couple should have. I highly recommend it."

J. Stewart Black,
Professor of Global Leadership and Strategy at INSEAD

"Bravo to the authors for writing this exceptional handbook. Grounded in the latest research, written from personal experience and peppered with real-life examples, this book is a must-read for International Career Couples and employers alike. It offers practical insights, tools and tips for ensuring that couples can cultivate a shared vision, nurture a secure space for open dialogue and ensure clarity around mutual career development."

Susan Goldsworthy OLY, Professor Leadership & Organizational Change, IMD; Co-author of three award-winning books.

"For couples who jointly embark on an international career journey this book will serve as a powerful resource for structuring important conversations and making vital decisions."

Konstantin Korotov, Professor of Organizational Behavior, Faculty Lead Executive MBA, ESMT Berlin

"This book takes readers by the hand on the path of a new but very current topic that is turning out to be of a greater relevance for international couples, recruiters and workers all over the world. The clarity and passion of the authors makes the reading fluent and never closing into clichés. Written in a confident style, the book features a clever analysis, supporting practical tools and incorporates real-life examples. It simply deserves to be read."

Paolo Boccardelli,
Professor and Dean Luiss Business School.

"The International Career Couple Handbook is among the most valuable contributions to the discussions on global talent mobility that I have seen in years. It has provided me with tangible and practical advice as to how I can improve my support to ICCs in the future. It provides well-researched and best practices to help ICC's take decisions and plan for a sustainable future together. It brings together the unique knowledge and experience that the authors have accumulated through decades of working with ICCs: A must-read read for anyone supporting a global workforce."

Lone Skriver,
Global Mobility Consultant

"As a leader in a knowledge intensive organisation specialised in change management we depend on international talent to serve the needs of our clients worldwide. The International Career Couple Handbook *underscores the wealth of talent among globally mobile employees and partners. Their global mindset and unique set of competencies are attractive to any employer serving global customers. As part of a dual-career couple myself, I applaud the authors for taking the subject to the next level, i.e. internationally mobile dual careers. The book offers spot-on advice for organisations to embrace and support this special talent base strategically."*

Caroline Mørck Jensen,
CEO Nexum Group

"Over the years I've seen many careers or couples derail because of the messiness of building an international life as a working couple. Paul and Jannie's book bring valuable insights and rare practical exercises for international career couples (and professionals who support them) to "unmess" that process. A workbook that has arrived in due time!"

Rafael Altavini,
Consultant and Leadership Advisor, Egon Zehnder

"My own international HR career happened in a traditional model of expatriation. Fast forward two decades and it's exciting to see how those with an international paradigm can now better prepare themselves as an international career couple. The frameworks and exercises in the handbook enable a pathway for the couple to navigate and negotiate how they can thrive internationally, professionally and personally, often within a family framework. This is a personal, self-managed guidance system. This handbook would have been invaluable at the beginning and indeed, throughout my international career journey."

John Rason, Group Head of Consulting, Santa Fe Relocation

"This book is extremely relevant and will just continue to be so as the world is globalizing and people meet across borders and boundaries. It feels that as part of evolution we keep meeting people with whom we have a common purpose and with whom we might yet be different from in terms of country in which we grew up in. Travelling the world and exploring it together is not only exciting and a way to learn, it can also be challenging when our careers is what moves us. This book brings you insights from the authors who besides having researched the topic, have lived it too. Go get your copy."

Kristin Engvig, Founder and CEO,
WIN Women's Global Leadership Journey

For Joseph
May he have the opportunity to explore the world.

For Sophia, Linus and Malika
Here to grow, love and learn!

CONTENTS

23	**Chapter 1 – Here We Are Starting From: Dual Careers in an Interconnected World**
24	WHAT IS AN INTERNATIONAL CAREER COUPLE?
29	INTERNATIONAL CAREER COUPLES: A GROWING PHENOMENON
	International Careers
	Dual Careers
	Women's Careers
37	WHY WRITE ABOUT INTERNATIONAL CAREER COUPLES?
	Risks and Opportunities for Organisations
40	WHAT YOU WILL FIND IN THIS BOOK
42	BEFORE YOU START
45	**Chapter 2 – Here's What We Know: Research on International Career Couples**
46	RESEARCHING THE INTERNATIONAL CAREER COUPLE
47	CHALLENGES FOR DUAL CAREER COUPLES
	How Do Dual Career Couples Meet Their Challenges?
	What Are the Keys to Success for Dual-Career Couples?
	What Can Employers Do for Dual-Career Couples?
	To Sum It Up: What Does Research Tell Us That's Relevant for ICCs?

60	HERE IS WHAT WE FOUND IN OUR RESEARCH
	Research Questions
	A Survey of International Career Couples
	Our Survey Participants
	Our Key Findings
	Critical Success Factors
	Interviews with International Career Couples
80	KEY TAKEAWAYS FROM CHAPTER 2
85	**Chapter 3 – Here We Are Going: Vision and Success Strategies For the International Career Couple**
86	VISION, STRATEGY AND THE ICC
	International Mobility as a Goal in Itself
	International Mobility as a Means to Achieve an End
	It Takes More Than One Conversation
91	VISION: MAPPING YOUR FUTURE AS ICC
	Creating Your ICC Vision
98	STRATEGY: SCENARIO PLANNING
	Three Important Conversations to Develop Scenarios
105	KEY TAKEAWAYS FROM CHAPTER 3
110	**Chapter 4 – Here We Are Becoming: The Identity of the International Career Couple**
112	WHAT IS AN ICC IDENTITY?
	How the ICC Identity is Distinct
115	WHY IDENTITY MATTERS FOR AN ICC

119	FINDING AND BUILDING AN ICC IDENTITY
	Identity Categories
125	CONSTRUCTING YOUR OWN ICC IDENTITY
	ICC Identity Exercise
	Your Origins as a Couple
129	KEY TAKEAWAYS FROM CHAPTER 4
135	**Chapter 5 – Here We Change: Sustaining the International Career Couple Over Time**
137	SECURE SPACE
	Secure Space Exercise
139	SECURE BASE AND MUTUAL CAREER DEVELOPMENT
	Mutual Career Development Exercise
148	STAKEHOLDERS
	ICC Stakeholder Mapping
156	KEY TAKEAWAYS FROM CHAPTER 5
161	**Chapter 6 – Here We Are Developing: Human Resource Management in the International Career Couple**
162	ICC KEY COMPETENCIES, VALUES, AND THE ENVIRONMENT YOU NEED
	ICC TimeLine Exercise

16	INTERNATIONAL COMPETENCIES
	Competency Development Exercise
173	EXTERNAL HUMAN RESOURCES: YOUR SUPPORTERS
175	CONTEXT
175	KEY TAKEAWAYS FROM CHAPTER 6
183	**Chapter 7 – Here We Are Talking: Handling Day-to-Day Complexity in the International Career Couple**
	ROLE MAPPING®: WHO DOES WHAT
	Role Mapping® Exercise
190	TALKING MEANS DIALOGUE
197	KEY TAKEAWAYS FROM CHAPTER 7
201	**Conclusion – Here We Stop**
204	**Bibliography – Here Is What We've Read**
208	**So, Here We Are: About the Authors**
	Paul Vanderbroeck: life and career
	Jannie Aasted Skov-Hansen: life and career

PREFACE

Our collaboration, which kicked off two years before we finished this final project, is itself an example of the beauty of international living. We met through a network connection, which underscores one of this handbook's main messages: Opportunities arise when you pursue your long-term vision and short-term goals on a global development path—while remaining open to unexpected turns. What's more, we were ahead of our time, in that we'd been working virtually well before the COVID-19 pandemic.

This book is grounded in our personal experiences as partners in International Career Couples, our encounters with the many couples we've befriended during our respective stints as expatriates, and our exchanges with talented individuals in our professional roles. From these engagements we learned, first separately and then as a team, that International Career Couples:

- are distinct from other dual-career couples;
- are not getting the support they need and deserve—from employers, publications or coaches;
- provide an opportunity for international talent management;
- are a complex organisation;
- can be successful and sustainable if they apply best practices from organisations.
- After coming together as a team, we saw it as our mission to provide the support International Career Couples need—and to show employers the opportunities in leveraging this talent. Our aim: Provide practical, easy-to-use solutions that such couples currently lack. At the same time, we wanted to not only ground our advice in our personal and professional experiences, but also to research what really works in International Career Couples.

All of this effort allowed us to develop for International Career Couples a sound method that combines multiple tools and exercises. Some we developed ourselves; others we adapted for International Career Couples from concepts that we'd found to be useful in our coaching and organisational development practices.

This handbook serves to empower International Career Couples to create a bright future in which international mobility, two fulfilling careers, a happy relationship, and perhaps a lovely family form a powerful mix. It is our sincere hope to inspire you—whether you're part of an ICC, or working with internationally mobile people, or otherwise interested in caring for a global workforce.

"Caring" really is a key word for us. Caring for yourself, your partner and the precious unity you are as an International Career Couple. Caring for your employees and their loved ones and, thus, for your organisation and its future globally mobile employees. Caring for the next generation of young professionals whom we all wish to see live happy, meaningful, influential lives. Finally, take it from us: An International Career Couple is difficult, doable and lots of fun!

Many people have contributed to this project. We thank our spouses for staying with us, so that after the book went to print, we could still safely claim to be part of an International Career Couple. Joking aside, Joëlle and Thomas each have, in their own way, given us support and inspiration, for which we are immensely grateful. We thank the International Career Couples who participated in our survey, especially the four couples who agreed to share their challenges, ambitions and stories with us. We thank our designer Anne Bundgaard, and our editor Steven DeMaio, for making this book attractive and easy to understand.

We, as authors, are of course fully responsible for the content. We also thank Jo Parfitt and Jack Scott, our publishers, for their help and sage advice. Finally, a big thanks to Artur and Madina Umerkaev, who noticed that independently of each other we were working on similar projects—and had the brilliant idea to bring us together.

An individual word of thanks from Paul: I thank the Women in Leadership Committee of the MBA class of 2016 at IMD Business School, especially Elena Olivi and Anupama Kateja. They invited me to do a workshop with the MBA class and their partners, allowing me to test my initial ideas. I'm grateful for the feedback I received, and for the hopes and fears they shared with me. Thanks also to my daughter Magdalena, who may be part of an ICC in the making, for her feedback on the manuscript. I am also indebted to the many coaching clients and fellow coaches who have consistently encouraged me to make this project happen.

An individual word of thanks from Jannie: My heartfelt thanks to all of the fantastic members of HERE WE ARE GLOBAL who contribute to our vibrant community and are passionate about building and sharing competencies in an interconnected world. On my journey as an entrepreneur, I am grateful to everyone who believes in and cheers me on to live out a fulfilling dual-career.

Paul Vanderbroeck
Jannie Aasted Skov-Hansen
Geneva, Copenhagen November 2020

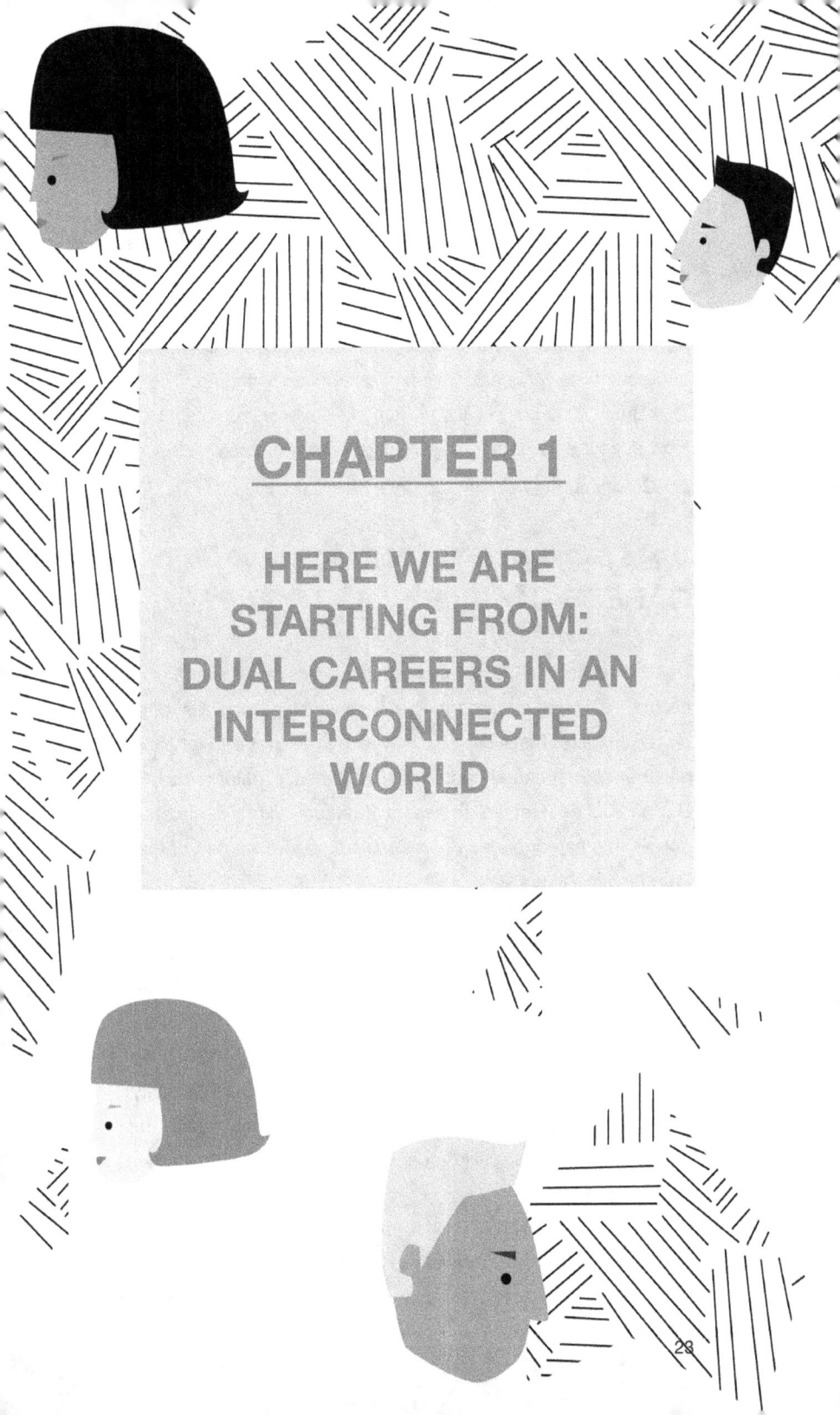

CHAPTER 1

HERE WE ARE STARTING FROM: DUAL CAREERS IN AN INTERCONNECTED WORLD

Suppose you're reading this book as a partner in an International Career Couple. You may not realize it yet, but there are many other couples out there like you—and your numbers are growing across the world. Suppose you're a leader in an organisation that depends on internationally mobile talent. In that case, this introduction will help you understand how this part of your workforce is changing.

But what exactly is an International Career Couple, or ICC? How does it differ from other types of career couples? And why do ICCs need their own (hand)book? We'll show you.

WHAT IS AN INTERNATIONAL CAREER COUPLE?

To define the ICC, we must first explain what it is and what it's not. It's also important to acknowledge that ICCs often remain invisible. That's because they tend to be mistaken for either a standard dual-career couple or a traditional expatriate couple. But an ICC does share an essential feature with a dual-career couple: the career of each partner is a fundamental part of their individual identities.

Notably, both ICCs and dual-career couples differ from dual-earner couples. In dual-earner partnerships, one career is valued more and therefore takes precedence over the other. That doesn't necessarily mean that each partner in a dual-career couple earns the same level of income. As in any dual-career couple, an ICC's partners may have a large income disparity, as, say, between an investment banker and a civil servant. But dual-career couples, unlike dual-earner couples, value the two careers equally.

Nevertheless, an ICC isn't just a dual-career couple who has moved to a different country. For an ICC, mobility is integral to the couple's identity—not a mere requirement or by-product of career development, as is often the case for other dual-career couples. ICCs see international mobility as part of who they are as they chart their road to success. This perspective may arise unexpectedly, when they're moved abroad by one of the partner's employers, or it might have been one reason the couple came together in the first place.

> "Joëlle and I have been forming an ICC for more than 20 years. One of the reasons I fell in love with her is our shared interest in exploring the world by working and living in different countries. Fate had it that we met at Geneva Airport. (If you're interested in the full story: I parked next to Joëlle, who had locked the keys inside her car. I drove her home to get the spare keys. The rest is history.)"
>
> Paul [author]

Distinguishing an ICC from a traditional expatriate couple is useful both for the ICC itself and for the partners' employers. That's because, in an ICC, it can happen that one partner's career is temporarily disadvantaged while the couple is on assignment, even though (in the long run) that career does not diminish in importance to the affected partner or the couple. If however, for an extended period, one partner has subordinated his or her own career to the other partner's, possibly with ensuing financial dependency, there's a structural imbalance. Thanks to the relationship, the couple may well be happy and sustain-able — and have one successful career. In such cases, some ICCs may persist in believing they're a dual-career couple. But for all intents and purposes, they've become a traditional couple, with a consistent primary breadwinner.

Different types of professional couples

	Committed to Single Career	Committed to Two Careers	Internationally Mobile
Single Earner Couple	√		
Expatriate Single Earner Couple	√		√
Dual Earner Couple	√		
Expatriate Dual Earner Couple	√		√
Dual Career Couple		√	
International Career Couple		√	√

The success and longevity of an ICC depend on different factors than those for traditional expatriate couples and dual-career couples (more on that in *Chapter 2—Here's What We Know*). Recent publications teach us that sustaining a dual-career couple over time is difficult indeed. In more than half of cases, the couples end up compromising one career in favour of the other, transforming themselves into a dual-earner or a single-earner couple, often because of challenges with (international) mobility. As defined by management scholar Liisa Mäkelä in her co-authored article "The role of expatriates' spouses among dual-career couples", a dual-career couple has two people who are psychologically committed to their professions, in which they have typically invested heavily as their primary source of self-fulfilment. The ICC is an internationally mobile dual-career couple and, therefore, inherently more complex.

Building on Mäkelä's definition, we define the ICC as:

> "An International Career Couple is a couple whose partners are psychologically committed to their professional careers (in which they have typically invested heavily as the primary source of self-fulfilment) and for whom international mobility is essential for the career success of one or both partners."
>
> Jannie and Paul [authors]

INTERNATIONAL CAREER COUPLES: A GROWING PHENOMENON

Three mutually reinforcing trends are causing ICCs to grow in number: international careers, dual careers, and women's careers. Each category is becoming more common and, thereby, boosting the numbers of the other categories.

Growth of ICC's Results from 3 Trends

© Paul Vanderbroeck / Jannie Aasted Skov-Hansen

International Careers

The 21st century is a global century. Never before have we witnessed so many goods and services—and with them, people—move across borders. Regional cooperation and international agreements have allowed people to move around more freely than ever before. Harmonisation of university degrees has made it easier to recruit foreign talent. Some sectors, such as academic research, have been almost entirely globalised. English has become virtually the only language in which researchers publish their findings.

Organisations in all sectors find staff mobility and international recruitment to be strategically important. More and more individuals have the ambition to seek employment in other countries, or to increase their career opportunities when they work internationally. Some 703 professionals responsible for Global Mobility programmes and who manage almost 700.000 expatriates expect these numbers to grow by double digits in the near future (Santa Fe Relocation 2019).

Apart from traditional organisation-sponsored international assignments, global careers are also made by individuals on their own initiative. Exchange programmes, such as Erasmus in Europe, and international MBA programmes all over the world have provided a platform for talented individuals to launch a global career. Younger generations, according to Santa Fe Relocation, are interested in continuing their education on the job. This includes international experience, which they expect employers to provide. More people moving abroad means more families and couples moving abroad.

"I've always been interested in living outside the Netherlands. I went to France and the USA to do research for my PhD. After that, I looked for an employer that offered opportunities to work in different countries. That's why I joined Royal Dutch/Shell. I was happy when, after two years, they sent me to Germany as an expatriate HR Manager."

Paul [author]

International Career Couples post-COVID-19

The data we've been using are from before the pandemic hit the world in 2020. Will this pandemic turn international mobility upside down? Global mobility is generally expected to decline as a result of COVID-19, as it has become more costly and risky for organisations.

The economy aside, the number of self-initiated expatriations shouldn't decrease as much as traditional expatriations do. For throughout humanity, danger has never stopped people from seeking opportunity elsewhere or helping other human beings in a different country.

For sure, globalisation has taken a hit as a result of the virus. But at the same time, the pandemic has acutely shown the need for international collaboration. Some organisations will still need to expatriate staff or recruit talent abroad. When every expatriate counts, employers will need to be very selective in choosing whom to expatriate. And those selected will have to be very talented and high-performing to yield a maximum return on investment for the employer.

To find those rare individuals and to be competitive, organisations can no longer afford to select mostly men. They'll have to source from the entire talent pool. And women, more often, bring along a career husband, thereby increasing the number of ICCs. If not this opportunity to find the best talent, then what else will prompt organisations to tackle the ICC challenge? This handbook can be part of the solution in facilitating global talent mobility post-COVID-19.

Dual Careers

Recent studies show that the number of dual-career couples is increasing: See, for example, data provided by INSEAD professor Jennifer Petriglieri *(Couples That Work)* and business author Avivah Wittenberg-Cox ("Being a two-career couple requires a long-term plan"). It's a generational development as well as the result of 'assortative mating', which is the tendency of people with similar outlooks and levels of education and ambition to marry each other. During the past three decades, assortative mating has risen by almost 25%, says Petriglieri. Consequently, fewer men have a female partner who's willing to give up her career to follow her husband. More people moving abroad means more dual-career couples moving abroad. If these couples continue on an international track and manage to develop both careers, they become ICCs.

Women's Careers

Twice as many female as male leaders are in a dual-career relationship, according to McKinsey. At the same time, women are increasingly moving into senior and professional careers, including international careers. When just looking at expatriates, the number of female assignees rose from 25% in 2018 to 32% in 2019, according to the Santa Fe Relocation survey. The conclusion is obvious: More women moving abroad means more dual-career couples moving abroad.

"When marrying Thomas, I knew that part of his career development would entail living and working in developing countries. I, too, wanted to explore new countries; I just hadn't found the right occasion to do so. We met during my studies, and decided to make it my opportunity as well to go to Nepal before finishing my bachelor's degree in Organisational Psychology. Since then I've always been adding relevant international work experience to my portfolio as an HR professional, specialising in global careers and emerging markets."

Jannie [author]

Gender and the International Career Couple

When doing the survey for our research on ICCs (see Chapter 2 — *Here's What We Know*), we noticed something about those survey participants who had responded to a call on social media (people neither of us knew before). In all cases but one, it was the woman who contacted us on behalf of the couple. After the survey, we asked follow-up questions to all participants: the social media respondents and the members of our network we'd invited to participate. When we did get a response to the follow-up from opposite-sex couples, it was always the woman who emailed us the couple's answers.

It couldn't be a coincidence, we thought. Intrigued, we looked for an explanation, and we noticed that research on dual careers is generally done by female academics. When linking this observation to data on international mobility, we can shed further light on the apparent eagerness of women to deal with the challenges of their ICC.

Here's an example from France, which traditionally

sends many expatriates into the world, in both the private and public sectors. Alix Carnot, a specialist on women and expatriation *(Chéri(e) on s'expatrie!),* surveyed 3500 French expats in 2015. A whopping 91% were men, most often followed by their female spouses. (In 2019 the French number was 92%. Globally, according to Santa Fe Relocation, the male proportion is closer to 68%).

Carnot's survey shows that two-thirds of the partners felt that they had made a significant career sacrifice in order to follow their spouse. These partners were mostly women, who had followed their husbands and had taken a hit on their careers. About half have found work, but not necessarily allowing them to continue their careers. For many, it's a demotion in terms of salary or hierarchical position. Few have received help from anyone. Among the partners who followed their spouses, 72% are university graduates (82% in NetExpat's 2018 international survey). The figures from other countries, with men as the vast majority of expatriates, are not substantially different.

Sometimes it can be a good idea in the lifetime of an ICC for one partner to temporarily step back. But unless the couple has a clear strategy, when push comes to shove (i.e., when the next move happens), it's often the same career that has the upper hand. As a result, lots of books and blogs are written, with the best intentions, usually by female partners who have undergone this experience themselves to help the expatriate partner 'cope' and develop 'their niche', sometimes claiming that money and financial independence are 'not everything'. Many of these publications give excellent practical tips and are worth reading. But even if they do reflect the current reality, they're not future-oriented. Given the statistics, you get easily lulled into the false belief that the traditional model of a male expat with a trailing spouse is the only avenue to happiness and success. We firmly believe that this doesn't do justice to ICCs. The women taking the initiative to sign their couple up for our survey agree with that.

And then there are women who avoid getting to this point in the first place, by compromising on their international mobility or on the relationship. Being in a couple or having a family stops women from accepting a geographical move much more often than it stops men, most likely because talented women tend to marry talented men. The NetExpat survey shows that 10% more women than men refuse an international assignment because of their partner's career. And high-achieving women divorce about twice as often as men, or simply stay single, according to a study from the University of Illinois (Wilson: "Keeping women in business"). Divorce is significantly more common in marriages where a promotion puts the wife ahead of the husband rather than the other way around, writes Derek Thompson in *The Atlantic* ("When a promotion leads to divorce"). For women who are offered an expatriation, the risk to their career or their couple is likely to exceed the risk for local dual-career couples.

That's when it clicked for us. Women were acting as the spokesperson of their ICCs in our survey not because of the stereotypical notion that wives are more concerned than husbands about the couple's relationship. Rather, these women made a rational, strategic choice to get support when they needed it—as women in a dual-career couple who want to be internationally mobile are at risk of either compromising their career to save the relationship or of breaking up the couple to save their career. And they know that their employers won't help them. These women are looking for support to integrate international mobility with a successful career for both partners in a couple that endures. This handbook offers precisely that type of support.

WHY WRITE ABOUT INTERNATIONAL CAREER COUPLES?

ICCs are a growing phenomenon, but available data cannot pinpoint the exact number. Earlier we explained that ICCs are hidden in the statistics on expatriates and dual-career couples. Even more relevant: ICCs present risks and significant opportunities for individuals and organisations alike.

Given our personal experience as ICCs, as well as our work in global mobility consulting and executive coaching, we know that being part of an ICC can be immensely fulfilling. At the same time, it's very challenging for both partners. Yvonne McNulty, a researcher specialising in international mobility, has studied 'trailing spouses', as well as marriage success, among expatriate couples. Participants in her studies have perceived professional support for a dual-career and social support (to alleviate marital stress) as the two factors that most significantly affect identity reconstruction and, in turn, adjustment—much-needed help that these expatriate couples do not get from their employers. Expatriate couples do divorce, but not in moresignificant numbers than other couples. The reason for the divorce, however, is often linked to the move abroad: either the move puts additional tension on a pre-existing issue, or the new culture causes difficulties for one or both spouses.

We believe that we can help ICCs reach the fulfilment they seek and deserve. An ICC is too complex to try to make it work without a methodological approach, or with methods that apply to other types of couples. ICCs are asking for such support (see sidebar on Gender and the ICC). This book provides the tools for couples to construct their future as a sustainable and successful ICC.

Risks and Opportunities for Organisations

Employers consistently underestimate both the risks and the opportunities ICCs bring to international talent management. Not distinguishing ICCs from other employees who cross borders with a spouse is not forward-looking; it orients employers' actions and policies toward perpetuating the status quo. And it certainly doesn't help to advance those talented women who want an internationally mobile career. Consequently, it prevents organisations from leveraging 100% of the talent pool for international staffing.

Surveys of organisations that employ expatriates, as well as of expatriates themselves (for example, by Net Expat, Permits Foundation, and Santa Fe Relocation), consistently show that the number-one reason employees refuse a move abroad is concern for possible negative consequences for the spouse's career. And when they nevertheless move abroad, the partner's unhappiness is the most common reason for a failed assignment or an early return. Although we've been unable to find pertinent data, we expect that it's similar for professionals who wish to pursue a career in a different country on their own, also known as 'self-movers'. Maybe more so for self-movers, because they often don't benefit from the same level of relocation support that employers provide to expatriates.

Employers' support for ICCs, mentioned in various publications, is limited only to short-term, single-assignment efforts. The employers tend to focus on making one individual— the employee—mobile for a particular assignment. Even when a menu of choices is available, policies favour one-size-fits-all support, usually tailored to 'trailing' homemakers or secondary-career partners, not full-career partners. Support mainly concerns cross-cultural and language training, information about local networks and social activities, and local job-hunting support.

Longer-term career support, as well as a focus on the couple as a whole, is lacking. A recent InterNations survey of 18,135 expatriates found that more than half received some kind of practical relocation support for accompanying spouses. Many would like even more help, particularly around networking. Whereas 90% of organisations in the NetExpat survey offer some assistance to partners who follow their spouses, it is far from enough: Employees and partners in the same study indicated that they were frustrated with the help they received from the expatriate's employer. Women expatriates in the UK oil industry, interviewed by Susan Shortland from the University of Westminster, have expressed frustration about the lack of understanding and support that their employers show for their career husbands.

Many organisations, unfortunately, see the problem but miss the opportunity. They try to circumvent the issue rather than solve it. Santa Fe Relocation's survey shows that organisations are trying to offer more and more short-term assignments without expatriating the whole family. Whereas this may make individuals internationally mobile for a short time, it does so at the expense of putting a burden on the expatriate and the family. What's more, it doesn't offer a long-term solution over the course of a career. In this way, local organisations are forced to accept a short-time expatriate for development reasons. They miss out on the added value of a long-term contribution. We doubt whether this is really the way to go to grow talent for international responsibilities—or to be sufficiently attractive for talent who explicitly want to move internationally.

Solving the ICC challenge, therefore, first reduces a costly risk factor for employers, by reducing the number of failed expatriations. Second, it provides the opportunity of increasing the talent pool of internationally mobile staff.

WHAT YOU WILL FIND IN THIS BOOK

- In *Chapter 2—Here's What We Know,* we summarise our own and others' research. We intended to discover what makes an ICC successful and sustainable. The conclusions have led us to develop a methodology for ICCs, which we explain subsequently.

"For organisations, it's time to rethink global career paths. It's time to look beyond the functional aspects of a mobile workforce and acknowledge what's going on in the personal space whenever a person decides to move to a new country for a job or career opportunity. As human beings, we all seek meaningfulness in our actions, and moving across borders must make sense for employees, self-movers and their partners alike. Everyone—mobility specialists, leaders and talent-acquisition partners—needs to come to terms with the new reality. Employee experience matters. Thoughtful solutions matter. And vibrant, dynamic, positive examples of a thriving global workforce are required to fuel the journey. With this book, we are here to turn issues into opportunities: To rewrite the story of dual global careers!"

Jannie [author]

- In *Chapters 3–7*, we systematically help you map your future as a successful and sustainable ICC.
  - This book is presented as a handbook. Therefore, it's filled with exercises. It's also illustrated with case studies from our research and our personal experiences.
  - As a couple, you can do the exercises on your own as a couple with the instructions provided. Going through all the exercises will take about 10 hours. We therefore suggest doing it on a weekend away, just the two of you in a place where you can work relaxed and undisturbed. However, you may already be well under way as an ICC. In that case, you may prefer to pick and choose from the exercises to complete your plans.
  - Should you want more support, you can download work sheets from www.herewareglobal.com. The worksheets are designed to facilitate the exercises.
  - If you seek even more support, you can also book coaching sessions for your ICC at the website.
- As an employer, you can show empathy for staff who are members of an ICC by giving them access to this handbook. Or you can use it to stimulate and facilitate your talent's international mobility by responding to the specific needs of ICCs.
- This book is mainly strategically oriented and focuses on what's different for the ICC. The *Conclusion* refers to www.herewareglobal.com, the point of entry for all practical questions about international mobility—and to a community of internationally mobile professionals across the world.
- References to research and other publications are mentioned as they come up throughout the book. The *Bibliography* at the end provides full references.

BEFORE YOU START

Let's conclude this chapter by sharing our goals and convictions in writing this book:

- To accord ICCs the unique position they deserve.
- To show that two partners can lead their ICC to sustainable success: An ICC is an organisation and works best when organisational best practices are applied to it.
- To empower you as an ICC in finding and developing your own best solution: ICCs don't need to be led by the hand, but they can benefit from learning and adapting a method that allows them to realise their ambitions.
- To show that being an ICC is a challenge and a choice worth considering.

YOUR NOTES

CHAPTER 2

HERE'S WHAT WE KNOW: RESEARCH ON INTERNATIONAL CAREER COUPLES

RESEARCHING THE INTERNATIONAL CAREER COUPLE

Compared with other professional couples, ICCs face greater complexity in building and sustaining a successful relationship. Given that complexity, we sought to go beyond the anecdotal evidence—of our personal ICC experiences and our professional encounters with other ICCs—and uncover what the research shows. Then we conducted our own investigation.

Our first step was to review the pertinent published research. But it turns out there isn't much of it. What does exist focuses primarily on the distinct topics of 'dual-career couples' and 'international mobility'. In this chapter, we summarise the existing research, when it's relevant to ICCs, but it offers at best a fraction of the answers we were seeking. That's because ICCs face unique, intersecting challenges related to dual careers and international mobility—not concerns that pertain to only one or the other. Much of the available research focuses on dual-career couples (without the international component), so we'll start there.

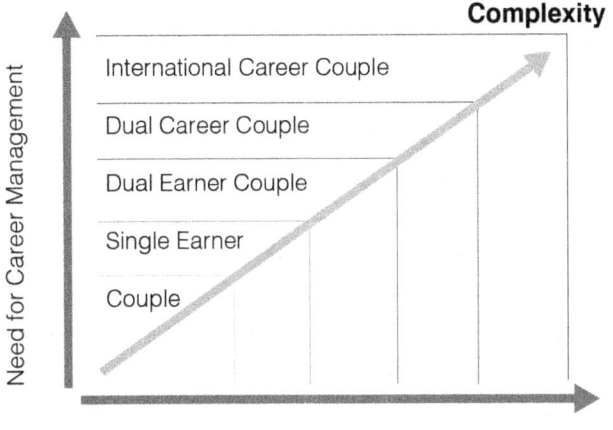

CHALLENGES FOR DUAL-CAREER COUPLES

According to INSEAD professor Jennifer Petriglieri *(Couples That Work)*, dual-career couples face two main challenges: flexibility and mobility. They find it tough to combine family life with inflexible working hours and commitments. Physical presence (or, since COVID-19, being online during fixed hours) is a factor that positively affects promotability. Mobility becomes a dilemma when one of the partners plans or gets a career-related offer to move to a different geographical location. This problem is made worse because companies (still) plan their staff moves for talent based on single-career households.

Petriglieri identifies three transitions that dual-career couples must undergo during a lifetime. The first is from two independent careers to two interdependent ones, triggered by a significant life event, such as moving into a joint home, a career

"When I was working for GM Europe, I was charged with recruiting MBAs to work in Marketing and Finance. Their first job was in the headquarters in Zürich, after which they would be moved to GM operations elsewhere. Often partnerships were formed with other MBAs in the office or with young GM expatriates from Germany or the US. When the next career move came up, the challenge of international mobility as a career couple was suddenly on the agenda. Neither the people concerned, nor the company, were really prepared for that. Some careers plateaued. Other people left. As a result, GM did not get as much out of these high-potentials as it could have."

Paul [author]

change, starting a family or a health issue. During this transition, the partners need to define and negotiate their respective roles in the couple. The couple must answer the question: How can we make this work?

The second transition Petriglieri calls 'reciprocal individuation'. This change stems from what some people characterize as a mid-life transition or crisis, involving fundamental doubts about whether to continue on a previous (career) path or start a new one. There's also a shift from following social demands and expectations, both professional and personal, to opening yourself up to your own needs and expectations. The couple faces the question: What do we actually want? They must help each other (reciprocity) as they each discover who they really are (individuation), thereby posing a threat to the personal relationship.

The third transition happens when couples reach senior levels of their careers or when children leave home or other commitments emerge, such as caring for elderly parents. The new reality requires reinvention and an answer to the question: Who are we now?

Each transition requires a fresh look at each partner's critical roles in the couple. New roles (for example, 'parent' when a child is born) must be integrated. And of course, roles may become less prominent over time (such as 'parent', once the nest is empty).

Executive coach Astrid Schreyögg looked at dual-career couples in Germany. Different roles (parent, professional, housemaker, partner, lover and so on) pose specific challenges. Some couples feel they have too many roles, or experience excessive tensions and conflicts among roles. Others would like to have a greater variety of roles. Still others find it challenging to make the transition from one role to another. Schreyögg raises an important point, in our view. The challenge of fulfilling different roles and transitioning between them poses a particular challenge to ICCs as well. To deal with this challenge, we've developed a method called RoleMapping®, which we'll present in *Chapter 7—Here We Are Talking.*

Finally, Yvonne McNulty, who has done a lot of research on expatriates, identifies four challenges specifically for ICCs in her co-authored article "A typology of dual-career expatriate spouses": practical/legal barriers (such as work permits and professional licences), lack of support from the expatriating organisation, marital stress, and the need to find a new professional and personal identity.

How Do Dual-Career Couples Meet Their Challenges?

Research on dual-career couples often distinguishes between successful and unsuccessful ones; categorizes the successful couples as one of four types, according to the solutions they've found; and assumes that to be successful, each dual-career couple must emulate one of those types. A couple who always prioritizes one career over the other is often considered to be a dual-career couple; Petriglieri, for example, calls them 'primary-secondary' couples. We deliberately classify this type of couple as a dual-*earner* couple, given that its challenges and solutions differ from those of a dual-career couple and, therefore, from those of an ICC. An ICC simply does not face the same realities as an 'expatriate with a trailing spouse', even if the spouse is somehow employed.

After excluding this type of couple, we're left with three main types of successful dual-career couples:

1. *Couples who pursue two separate, individual careers,* while investing heavily in logistics, child care, and hired help to manage family life. Different researchers call this type of dual-career couple by various names: 'dual male career' (Bathmann) or 'double primary' (Petriglieri) or 'parallelograms' (Wittenberg-Cox).
2. *Couples who alternate which partner's career takes precedence:* 'dual career–dual care' (Bathmann) or 'turn-taking' (Petriglieri) or 'alternators' (Wittenberg-Cox).

3. *Couples who actively aim for win-win situations* by developing career opportunities for each partner that positively influence the career of the other partner: 'co-preneurs' (Bathmann) or, 'complements' or 'mergers' (Wittenberg-Cox). This solution occurs, notably, when a career move requires a relocation—for instance, by ensuring that the new location offers good employment prospects for the partner.

What Are the Keys to Success for Dual-Career Couples?

Most couples in all three aforementioned types, identified by family researcher Nina Bathmann in her book on female careers in Germany, have a long-term view. These couples also tend to support each other in their respective careers. The result is that a partner in a profession with more challenging career prospects gets, on balance, more support for his or her career, thereby keeping both partners on equal footing in the long term. Such partners continuously give each other practical, emotional and motivational support for their respective work challenges. Some couples can tolerate temporary separations when they live in different locations.

Partners who positively benefit from being in a dual-career couple therefore feel that they've achieved more in their careers together than they could have done on their own. When these partners mutually support and encourage each other, they each find it easier to explore career opportunities. What's more, this dynamic can expand both partners' professional identities, whereby they incorporate positive attributes of the spouse's identity into their own (Petriglieri).

Petriglieri argues that dual-career couples should not rely too much on economic decision criteria to make essential choices, such as a location or a career move. It can lead to favouring one career over the other, permanently, thereby undermining the basic concept of a dual-career couple. Nor is it a good idea to make an essential decision—about life, career or location aspirations—while ignoring long-term consequences. She warns against focusing on merely solving obvious practical problems, as opposed to dealing with the fundamental underlying issues.

Petriglieri proposes using a regularly reviewed 'couple contract' to prevent potential pitfalls—by articulating common values, setting direction, specifying geographical and time boundaries, and identifying fears. In comparison, Bathmann recommends supporting each other's career objectives, aligning career steps early on, and supporting each other in professional matters. Further down we'll see that supporting each other professionally, and agreeing on a direction as a couple, are keys to the success of ICCs.

"Four years after our return from Nepal, my husband, Thomas, asked me to consider a second assignment — this time in Central Asia. My first instinct was: Asia and mountains, been there done that. Only after jointly discussing the benefits of leaving my corporate job behind, I immersed myself in learning Russian and further upgrading my HR skills. Encouraged by my partner in joy, I stepped up to become Chair of the Governing Board of an IB World School and acquired life and work experience I could have never come close to in Denmark. This was part of our joint vision to remain global citizens and teach our children the value of pushing boundaries and daring to take a leap of faith. As it were, I managed to return to the same company, Novo Nordisk, after 3,5 years in Kyrgyzstan. Partly, because I managed to show how I stayed relevant in my field and had expanded personally and professionally."

Jannie [author]

What Can Employers Do for Dual-Career Couples?

Bathmann's advice to employers remains, to a large extent, at the traditional level of offering relocation services. Rather than empowering the couple to construct what's best for them, she and her co-authors recommend measures to 'take care of' the so-called 'trailing spouse' when expatriation occurs. More helpful, from our perspective, is their demand for changing career paths to create less-restrictive time windows for vital career steps. Finally, Bathmann recommends that employers introduce part-time leadership positions, reduce the need for mobility in careers, and offer need-based benefits (cafeteria approach). McKinsey's dual-career initiative for its consultants mainly focuses on helping couples cope with and manage the current and near-term situation rather than offering a long-term perspective.

*"It happened to me.
As an expat in Germany for Shell, I started a relationship with a British expatriate (an Anglo-Dutch couple, how very 'Shell'). When I was repatriated to the Netherlands, my partner benefited from the same spousal support programme I'd helped to set up in a previous job. However, it was not enough and only addressed to her, not to us as couple. So, we turned things around and left Shell. We both found interesting jobs in Switzerland and moved there."*

Paul [author]

To Sum It Up: What Does Research Tell Us That's Relevant for ICCs?

Arguably, most if not all studies of dual-career couples offer recommendations that would apply equally to single-career or working couples. In all configurations of couples, it makes sense to focus on factors such as proper distribution of roles and responsibilities, basing important decisions on shared values, mutual emotional support, and reserving some 'couple time'.

Not least because of our personal experience as ICCs, we have our doubts about choosing and following a specific 'couple type' right up front. Such rigidity risks putting couples in a box and making them less likely to explore unknown territory. Besides, well into the 21st century, there is too much diversity in partnerships to fit them all into a few types. Still, it's useful for a couple to know that different approaches exist. It helps to structure your thinking when you're developing your strategy as an ICC, and it can be useful for calibrating your own solution. Nevertheless, it's crucial for ICCs to find their own approach and solution that suit their relationship, personalities and circumstances. What's more, this solution may well change over time. It's about the method, not the model.

> "...a marriage is its own sovereign state, with explicit contracts and implicit regulations, and the division of labor in couples of all ages is the domestic responsibility of the men and women within them."
>
> Derek Thompson,
> *The Atlantic*

Generally, research lumps ICCs together with local, not internationally mobile, dual-career couples. Is there nothing that distinguishes an ICC? Is wanting to achieve two rather than one primary career—and to do so internationally—merely another challenge? There is little research specifically on ICCs to address these questions. After interviewing expatriate career spouses, management scholar Agnieszka Kierner concluded that they start with a lot of hope only to end up disillusioned. A study by Marja Känsälä and other Finnish academics shows that ICCs, for lack of a better solution, tend to end up in one of three situations: One career takes precedence over the other; the two partners equally sub-optimise their careers; or they individually pursue two careers at the expense of family life or sharing a home. Irish scholar Margaret Linehan interviewed 50 female European top managers with an international career, who had originally started out as a dual-career couple. By the time of the interview, eight had divorced. The others had reverted to a primary-secondary or single-earner model. Many of these couples stay together and feel happy. Yet in our definition, these variations imply compromising rather than taking advantage of opportunities.

What, then, is a successful ICC? We believe that couples should themselves determine whether they're successful or not. But many couples seem to think their context is unchangeable; rather than pushing boundaries, they adapt and settle for less. Often, that means compromising one career or family life in order to save the couple. It's regrettable and a loss of potential for both the couple and their employers if the couple seeks to be successful only within given constraints. Instead, they should explore expanding options to reach a win-win solution rather than a compromise. But how do you make sure that the ICC is more than the sum of its parts? How do you make being part of an ICC add value to the couple, the two careers and the family? How do you get to 1+1=2+?

One final point before we turn to our own research: Expatriation adds to the complexity of a relationship within a dual-career couple. The number of women in senior careers is rising. Given the reality that career women tend to choose career partners more than the other way around, there's a particular strain on the international mobility of female talent. Helping ICCs succeed is therefore intrinsically connected to the career progression of women leaders and gender balance. So here it goes: Employers who don't want to miss out on female talent are well-advised to facilitate the mobility of ICCs.

"I met my first ICC-to-be in my first job for Royal/Dutch Shell. I was responsible for planning the careers of some 550 petroleum engineers and deploying them worldwide. Marion (pseudonym), one of the few women engineers, was in my population. Marion's next career step called for an expatriation. I found a suitable opportunity for her in the Middle East, as her specific skills would add much value to the local requirements. Given that Shell HR recently had set an objective to have more diversity among its expatriates, I saw my chance. The local Shell affiliate was keen on Marion, when I proposed her candidacy. The glitch was that she had a partner, Klaas (pseudonym). The three of us had a conversation. Marion and Klaas were willing to marry to...

... meet the local cultural norms, provided that Klaas could continue his business as a furniture designer. Together with my counterpart, a local national in HR, we managed to arrange everything. Then at the last moment, the local Managing Director called off the move. They were happy to have Marion, but only on her own. For a woman, it would already be a first. Even with his own business, her husband would be perceived as dependent on her — it would have been too much for the local culture to tolerate, I was told. I learned from this experience. In parallel, I was a member of a working group to update Shell's expatriate policies. I managed to get a pilot accepted to test out giving expatriate partners access to an outplacement service that helps them find a job."

Paul [author]

HERE'S WHAT WE FOUND IN OUR RESEARCH

Research Questions

After reviewing the existing literature, we set out to meet actual ICCs and do our own analysis of them, to fill the gaps in the current research. Our aim: Focus specifically on ICCs, not just dual-career couples in general. Also, most research on dual-career couples emphasises what goes wrong and sometimes proposes preventive remedies. Instead, we chose to explore what works. We've researched only success stories, to identify best practices.

An ICC is a small yet complex organisation. Sustaining it successfully requires best practices from the leadership of organisations. Love alone is not enough. Neither is proper management. We therefore hypothesized that, for ICCs to succeed, leadership is required: offering a long-term perspecive and making sure the organisation follows. These were our research questions:

- What really distinguishes an ICC from a dual-career couple?
- What do successful ICCs actually do, concretely?
- Do successful ICCs indeed find their own individual solution rather than fit into an existing type or model?

A Survey of International Career Couples

First, we questioned 30 ICCs using an online survey in November and December of 2019. These ICCs were either part of the respective network of the authors or responded to a call for participants through social media. We deliberately selected ICCs that had been successful and still were considered successful in terms of career, relationship, and international mobility at the time of the survey. When surveyed, all rated their progress as a couple overall as 'Satisfactory' at least; two-thirds even responded with 'Highly Satisfactory' or 'Fantastic'. The vast majority reported 'Satisfactory' or 'More than satisfactory' career progression. Only a few individuals nevertheless indicated some disappointment with their careers. Second, we interviewed four individual couples to investigate more deeply what works in ICCs.

Looking at these well-functioning couples has allowed us to identify what works rather than what makes ICCs fail. Our research confirmed some of what we'd read in previous publications and also revealed new, different perspectives. The insights from our research have been essential to our developing the tools and counsel found in this book. We summarise the results below and give some concrete examples. You'll find more examples as we discuss various topics later.

Our Survey Participants

The ICC seems to remain a phenomenon primarily of the West, with most of the research on European and North American couples. The majority of participants in our survey also originate from Europe or North America, but ICCs from developing countries participated, too. Half of our respondents are binational couples. A small minority are same-sex couples. Most of the surveyed ICCs are married, and two-thirds have children. Most live together. A few have a commuting relationship, whereby each partner lives in a different country. The sample we surveyed was genuinely international: two-thirds of respondents have relocated to a different country as a couple at least twice. They are mostly age 30 to 50. We looked at different durations of relationships, ranging from less than 5 years to more than 15 years.

We found that looking at economic sectors is not relevant, as ICCs have by definition two employers, which may be private sector, non-profit or public sector. More important, employment changes as people move and develop careers. Our survey is a snapshot of one moment in time. We did notice that three quarters of the individuals were employed in the private sector. For a travelling partner, it's probably easier to find (self)employment in the private sector in a different country. Because public sector organisations rarely recruit from abroad.

Here are the key statistics of the couples and individuals from our survey:

ICC SURVEY Demographics for Participant Couples

Age group	<30	30–40	40–50	>50
	7%	43%	43%	7%
Together as a couple	<5 years	5–10 years	10–15 years	>15 years
	20%	13%	20%	47%
Background of individual participants	Europe, North America, Australia	Africa	Asia	Middle East, Latin America
	81 %	5%	7%	7%
Number of relocations as a couple	0	1	2	>2
	3%	27%	20%	50%
Nationality of partners	same nationality		binational	
	57%		43%	
Married	yes		no	
	80%		20%	
Children	yes		no	
	70%		30%	
Composition	mixed sex		same sex	
	93%		7%	
Partners in same location	yes		no	
	87%		13%	

Our Key Findings

Couples with children and those without children gave similar responses about their level of happiness with their individual career advancement and with their overall success as a couple.

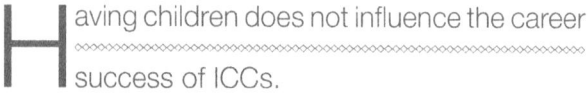

H aving children does not influence the career success of ICCs.

As expected, the career satisfaction of both partners appears to be an indicator of success for well-functioning ICCs. As we expected, our survey respondents rated their progress as a couple overall, with private and professional aspects combined, as 'Satisfactory', 'Highly Satisfactory' or 'Fantastic'.

Our survey uncovered other interesting correlations. First, the happier the two partners were with their careers, the more positively they viewed their partnership. Second, among couples who rated their progress as no better than 'Satisfactory', we found relatively more partners who believed that their relocation abroad had harmed their careers. Third, the more frequently the couple relocated to a different country, the less content they were about their progress as a couple over time. Two key findings emerged:

B oth partners' career satisfaction is critically important for the ICC's success.

International mobility is the most significant potential risk factor for career satisfaction of the following partner.

These findings also imply that potential expatriates are not exaggerating when they say they hesitate to accept a foreign assignment out of concern for their partner's career, as it really could put the couple at risk.

Our research reveals the magnitude of the challenge of sustaining a successful ICC through its various moves. This fact became clear to us early on, when several couples we were considering as potential participants split up before we could survey or interview them. And our personal experience also bears this out. (Twice, Paul [author] has been a partner in an ICC. The first one ran aground in part because of the difficulty of maintaining two careers while being internationally mobile.) Not surprisingly, each move takes a toll on the ICC. Despite being happy overall, including professionally, in one of every five couples we surveyed, one partner believed that the relocation abroad had been bad for his or her career. Overcoming the mobility challenge is of utmost importance for ICCs. That's where ICCs differ from other dual-career couples. Overcoming this challenge takes focus and effort—the very reason to write this book.

Our survey showed that getting the family settled is not a determining success factor for ICCs, despite the attention that expatriate policies typically give to relocating the family. Employers, therefore, would do well to treat ICCs differently from other expatriates and internationally recruited staff. ICCs become more mobile if the two partners are treated as a single entity rather than separate individuals. As the research discussed earlier shows, impediments to international mobility nowadays most often arise from the career situation of the partner who is more affected by the move and who, therefore, loses more. Employers often prioritize fixing the problem of the trailing spouse and are advised to do so by consultants and academics alike. Our findings lead us to challenge this approach in favour of one that prioritizes the couple rather than the individual.

> ICCs become more mobile if the partners are treated as a single entity rather than as separate individuals.

Appropriately, then, the couple must redefine its identity, rebrand itself, and jointly articulate its vision. Indeed, three-quarters of our ICC survey respondents claimed to have at least some form of a Shared Vision. The more the couple shares a vision, the less they typify themselves as having 'Two independent' careers. Said differently, the couples who qualify themselves as having 'Mutually supportive' or 'Alternating' careers all have a Shared Vision to at least some extent. Couples with some form of a vision are most of the time also those who have a ritual for important decisions, such as a job change or a relocation. A ritual might mean having crucial talks in a particular place or at a specific time, such as alone in the kitchen or bedroom, or at breakfast or on a date night.

And the vision is genuinely shared: the more an ICC has a Shared Vision, the more each partner feels responsible for the career success of the other partner, and the happier they are about their overall progress as a couple. What's more, having a structured approach to meaningful conversations helps: couples with a ritual are somewhat more satisfied with their overall progress as a pair than are those who do not hold such discussions at a particular time or place.

Although we want to avoid typecasting ICCs, we nevertheless included in our survey a question about different types of couples: half the couples currently managed 'Independent' careers; the other half had 'Alternating' careers or 'Mutually supportive' careers. The difference between the latter two is that, in the case of alternating careers, the partners switch back-and-forth whose career takes precedence; usually, this switch happens upon each relocation. In the case of mutually supportive careers, the two partners actively help each other to develop their careers in parallel.

In our survey, we found that the younger the couple, the more predisposed they were to having 'Mutually supportive' careers. This answer seems to imply that, from the outset, the partners have made a conscious choice to build on a foundation of equality.

Whatever their approach to careers, ICC partners feel that they're in this together. When asked individually, almost all respondents reported involving their partner 'In an important way' in critical career decisions, and most said they felt supported by their partner in job and career. Two-thirds indicated that they felt 'Very much' or 'Entirely' responsible for the career success of the other partner. Not surprisingly, we found this sense of responsibility more among ICCs with mutually supportive or alternating careers than among those who have two independent careers.

Digging down, we observed that the couples with mutually

supportive careers are the most positive about their progress as a couple—and about their individual career progress. Among those, we also found the most individuals who believe that their career has benefited from being with their partner.

> Mutual support in careers pays off in individual career success and in partnership success.

As the previously discussed research suggests, dual-career couples who move abroad frequently compromise the career of one partner to save the relationship. Our research shows that the first five years of the partnership are the critical window for finding a successful outcome on this issue. If success is not achieved during those years, the partners may still continue as a couple, but at the price of the career of one partner or by sacrificing international mobility. In four out of six couples who were together for fewer than five years, one partner felt that his or her career had suffered from relocating abroad— a clear red flag. These individuals believe they perhaps would have been better off, career-wise, without the partner or without moving. Could the support of these young couples for their partner's career be less effective than they hope it would?

"One of the experiences that inspired this book was my work with MBA students at, for example, IMD and INSEAD. I coached many of them through their journey, which is meant to be career-changing and, often, life-changing. If you do an international MBA, you generally start an international career. Some of the students I coached already had a partner; others met their partner in class. Regardless, for quite a few of them, the topic of internationally mobile dual careers was a priority as they neared completion of their MBA, when the job search is paramount. Some of them are in successful ICCs. I'm proud that they agreed to participate in our survey. One of my MBA coachees, after having met Jannie separately, immediately saw the connection between our ideas and brought us together."

Paul [author]

Half of the younger couples in our survey had two independent careers—about the same proportion as the older couples. Nevertheless, the younger couples overwhelmingly claimed that they support each other's careers and make no vital decisions without significant involvement of their partner. All of them reported believing that they have, to at least some extent, a Shared Vision as an ICC. So, despite a Shared Vision, Mutual Support, and joint career decision-making, most younger ICCs have a partner who is struggling with career concerns because of moving abroad. These younger couples know what's important but don't know how to achieve it. The subsequent chapters will focus on the how.

> Mutual support and knowing where to go are not enough to make an ICC successful. Knowing how to get there is equally important.

Couples with relationships of different durations were similar in their tendencies to share a vision, give mutual support, and have a specific ritual for making crucial decisions. We did find, however, that the longer the couple is together, generally the happier they are about their progress as a couple—all things (professional and personal) considered. These couples deserve to be proud of their achievement, in our view. It calls for a celebration!

Across age groups, the couples who have found a way to make it work stay together, specifically by compromising neither the couple's relationship nor the career of one partner. To sustain two careers, an ICC appears to face its most significant challenges at the beginning of the relationship and when decisions regarding relocation arise.

An ICC faces its most significant challenges at the beginning of the relationship and when decisions regarding relocation arise.

Our survey results confirm our hypothesis that it's worthwhile for ICCs to view themselves as an organisation or a team. Career development is vital for the success of any organisation. It is no different for ICCs. Couples generally coordinate their personal and family lives, but not necessarily their careers. We learned that when ICCs coordinate, their individual careers benefit more than when they manage careers separately. One of the ICCs in our survey (together for 25 years) gave the following advice: *"It's vital to clarify mutual ambitions and expectations from the get-go and then have regular check-ins and mutual support along the way."*

Seeing your ICC as a team is vital to sustaining the couple over time.

Because moving abroad distinguishes ICCs from other dual-career couples, we asked ICCs how international mobility affects their careers. We noted earlier that in one out of five couples we surveyed, one partner's career took a hit from relocating abroad, predominantly among ICCs that have two independent careers. Two-thirds to three-quarters of the partners in couples that have mutually supportive or alternative careers said that their career has benefited from moving abroad, compared with such benefit among only half the partners in ICCs with two independent careers.

Conversely, fewer than 15% of the couples with mutually supportive or alternative careers indicated having a partner whose career has suffered from moving abroad, compared with about 30% among ICCs with two independent careers. So, although love may be enough for the private side of the partnership, more is required for a successful career and a move abroad. In short, the partners' careers must also become a focus; the cooperation raises each partner's professional prospects and also helps to migrate careers across borders without disadvantage.

> Cooperation and mutual support of the two partners' careers sustain an ICC in the long term.

Critical Success Factors

Overall, we found that ICCs don't achieve success by following a predetermined template for the type of couple to be. Instead, they should use a method that focuses on one or more critical success factors (listed below) to arrive at their individual solution. This is really how an ICC ensures that the sum of 1+1 = 2+. We also found that what works for ICCs does not depend on whether the couple is expatriated by one partner's employer or has crossed borders on their own initiative. Besides, the distinction can become blurred over time. So, Jannie [author] has been twice expatriated through her husband's work. Paul [author], whose career spans a higher number of years, has been twice expatriated by his employer, and then moved to another country as a self-mover and is now expatriated as a result of his wife's job.

SHARED VISION
Develop the vision as early as possible: either an achievement to be attained in the long term or the fulfilment of a purpose that guides you throughout a lifetime.

SECURE SPACE
Settle on a ritual or process for making strategic decisions, calibrating thoughts and feelings, and sustaining the ICC over time.

MUTUAL CAREER DEVELOPMENT
Mutually support each other in developing and coordinating your individual careers, most notably when relocating to a different country.

Leadership of the ICC involves these elements:

- A *Shared Vision* to show the way.
- A *Secure Space* and *Mutual Career Development* to get the organisation to follow the direction by means of:
  - trust, motivation, and effective decision-making, developing the capabilities needed, and offering
  - opportunities for professional self-fulfilment

The case studies below exemplify how the four couples we interviewed are applying at least one of the three critical success factors.

Interviews with International Career Couples

Let's meet the four ICCs we interviewed, as their diverse experiences and our own inform the recommendations throughout this book. Having entrusted us with their intimate thoughts, feelings and experiences, the interviewees prefer to remain anonymous. We therefore use pseudonyms, while leaving all other data and details unchanged.

The four interviewed couples represent each relationship duration: <5 years, 5–10 years, 10–15 years, >15 years. Three couples are from Western developed countries; one is from a non-Western developing country. One of the four is a same-sex couple. Two of the four are classic expatriate couples; they moved abroad on the initiative of one partner's employer. The other two are internationally mobile on their own initiative. We interviewed each of the four ICCs as a couple, not each partner separately. The interviews took place in February and March of 2020, after we had the opportunity to analyse the results of the online survey.

ANTONELLA AND SERGIO

are a European couple, together for less than five years when we interviewed them. Antonella moved to Denmark for a job as Research Programme Manager. Sergio followed her and now works as a Management Consultant. This is their first move to another country, and it happened at their own initiative.

JOHN AND MARTIN

are married with two children. They've been together for more than five years. They moved to a different country twice on their own initiative. They met in Australia and moved to Europe, where Martin grew up. They're now back in Australia, where together they set up a business in Healthcare.

KASHAF AND ZAROON

have been together for more than 10 years, after having met in their home country in South Asia. Married with two children, they currently live in Central Asia. Zaroon works as a Finance Director in Education, seconded by the NGO he works for. Their family had been expatriated to Africa once before, also through Zaroon's employer. Kashaf has a job as an HR Consultant for two NGOs.

SILJE AND TIM

are a European couple together for almost 20 years. Married with two children, they recently were expatriated to Singapore through Silje's employer, a Food Science company. Silje is the Regional HR Director. Tim currently works in Singapore as a Business Process Manager in the Oil & Gas industry.

Kashaf and Zaroon's Shared Vision

Kashaf and Zaroon developed early on the vision to ensure a good retirement, which means having enough money so that their children do not need to take care of them in old age. Moving abroad was the condition to finance this retirement. Now, expatriated for a second time, the couple has adapted their vision to include allowing their children to benefit from an international education.

John and Martin's Shared Vision

John and Martin agreed that their children should have the same solid family upbringing that both enjoyed in their youth. This implies limited outsourcing of child care and always a parent at home. At the same time, they agreed that neither career should be disadvantaged. Hence, their vision has been to pursue alternating careers.

John and Martin's Secure Space

John and Martin have their crucial conversations in the evening in their living room when the kids are in bed. When they disagree, both nevertheless commit to the decision they have made together. The important thing is that each one's point of view has been heard. As a result, they rarely go back on a decision.

Kashaf and Zaroon's Secure Space

Kashaf and Zaroon plan a lot. They did much research before moving to their current country so that they could settle down quickly and easily. They have these important discussions while enjoying a cup of chai together at night, when the kids are sleeping.

Silje and Tim's Secure Space

Silje and Tim talk a lot, almost every day, often while taking a walk in the evening as the babysitter looks after the children. This time allows them to plan for the future and review their progress.

Antonella and Sergio's Mutual Career Development

When Sergio followed Antonella to her new country, Antonella helped him with his job applications, CV writing, networking and the like. Meanwhile, Sergio has become so good at this work that Antonella goes to him for support in professional networking.

Silje and Tim's Mutual Career Development

Silje and Tim's mutual support often goes beyond career development into general professional support. When both partners have complementary skills, they can help each other with the challenges they face at work. Silje relies on Tim's capabilities to prepare important presentations.

KEY TAKEAWAYS FROM CHAPTER 2

Starting in *Chapter 3 — Here We Are Going*, we'll help you develop the success factors for your own ICC. But first let's review what we've covered so far.

There is little research on International Career Couples (ICCs), as most available studies focus either on dual-career couples or internationally mobile couples.

This book relies mainly on our research on successful ICCs, as well as our personal and professional experience.

Successful ICCs rely on one or more of these key success factors: Shared Vision, a Secure Space for discussion and decision-making, and Mutual Career Development for both partners.

YOUR NOTES

CHAPTER 3

HERE WE ARE GOING: VISION AND SUCCESS STRATEGIES FOR THE INTERNATIONAL CAREER COUPLE

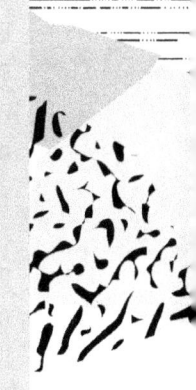

VISION, STRATEGY AND THE ICC

*I*f You Don't Know Where You Are Going, You'll Probably End Up Somewhere Else. The straightforward wisdom in David Campbell's 1974 book title, paraphrasing the Cheshire Cat from Lewis Carroll's Alice in Wonderland, is indisputable. Like any successful organisation, an ICC needs a clear sense of direction: a vision. As our research shows *(see Chapter 2 – Here's What We Know)*, having a Shared Vision is critical to an ICC's success. That vision articulates long-term career and mobility goals, as well as the fulfilment of a lifetime purpose (which may combine career and familial aims). This orientation toward what really matters allows the ICC to make big, future-oriented decisions with a strategic focus, rather than merely drawing from past experiences and responding to short-term demands.

The ICC's two equal partners share the leadership for developing and implementing their vision. They cooperate while dividing responsibilities, dynamically shifting authority, drawing from complementary talents and personalities, building on shared values, and setting ambitious yet realistic expectations. This chapter teaches you how to develop your own ICC's Shared Vision—and a strategy to get there. But first, let's consider some examples.

JOHN & MARTIN'S VISION

John and Martin, currently based in Australia, developed a threefold Shared Vision:

1. Offer a solid family to their children.
2. Don't compromise on either career.
3. Lead a full life.

Intense discussions before each crossroads led John & Martin to alternate playing the lead role in career versus parental care, while living together for a period in each of their respective countries. That approach allowed them and their children to experience each partner's culture and family, one at a time.

"Our vision has been to move—to work toward a good retirement, which means not having to rely on our children. We've made investments, buying land in our home country to make that happen. We want our children to have a good life. We started with little means. We had to borrow money for our marriage. At the same time, we want to have two careers."

Kashaf & Zaroon

International Mobility as a Goal in Itself

For some couples, the "I" in ICC — international — is a goal in itself, a deliberate aim. For other ICCs, international mobility is a means to an end: being a dual-career couple is the primary ambition, and the international component is the best way to realise it.

Let's take a typical situation when one partner's employer offers the opportunity to move abroad. A couple who sees international mobility as a goal in itself must assess whether this particular opportunity fits their long-term plan.

International mobility as a goal in itself

Antonella and Sergio, the youngest couple we interviewed, are such an example. Antonella dreamed of pursuing her career in life sciences in a new country. Once she got the opportunity to move to Scandinavia, Sergio jumped on the bandwagon. He's been enjoying the ride so much that he now sits in the driver's seat next to his wife to develop their international future.

International mobility as a goal in itself

Joëlle and Paul met after independently pursuing international careers, which made it easy for them to find ommon ground. They realised their shared goal of moving to a different country by cooperating to steer Joëlle successfully through the application process for her current job. Meanwhile, Paul has continued his career as an international consultant and author of the book you're reading now.

International Mobility as a Means to Achieve an End

For an ICC who views international mobility as a means to achieve success as a dual-career couple, the expatriation opportunity can come as a surprise.

International mobility as a means to an end

Our couple from South Asia, Zaroon and Kashaf, typify this example. When Zaroon's employer offered him a position in Africa, they already had a clear vision—for their children to have a good life and not have to care financially for their aging parents. Once expatriated, Zaroon and Kashaf discovered that an international career was the best way to achieve their Shared Vision.

International mobility as a means to an end

Silje and Tim had not thought of an international move until Silje's employer came up with an offer in Asia. The couple already had a guiding principle of 'all for one and one for all', such that important decisions were always family decisions. Staying flexible, by not being chained to a financial commitment or an employer, is fundamental for them. After seeing that moving to Asia would fit this overarching purpose, they said yes to the employer's offer.

It Takes More Than One Conversation

Being proactive allows an ICC to take their lives and careers into their own hands, to seize on the opportunities that fit their Shared Vision, and to be in a position to make the right decision once an opportunity arises. But articulating and arriving at a vision is difficult, because as soon as you decide to go somewhere, you risk the personal disappointment of not getting there and of potential social embarrassment. Some ICCs we interviewed mentioned that they feel competitive with other (expatriate) couples. On the one hand, this motivation pushes the ICC to make their couple and career work; on the other hand, if you don't make it, you have to face your friends and peers.

Developing a Shared Vision takes much thought and more than one heart-to-heart conversation. The process is challenging, even scary. It's difficult to clearly express what you feel and mean, to be heard by your partner and understood in the way you intend. A lot is at stake. (See *Chapter 7 – Here We're Talking* for guidance about dialogue.)

VISION: MAPPING YOUR FUTURE AS ICC

We've established that a Shared Vision is critical to an ICC's success. Now let's turn to how to develop one, using an instrument that will help. We call the process *Mapping the Future of Your ICC*, and throughout the rest of this book we'll show you how to use it and provide you with tools that help you fill it out.

You create this map yourself, for example using Power Point®. Or you could use a flipchart with sticky notes, or even pictures and clippings for illustration and inspiration. However you make the map, you'll change it over time as your relationship and careers evolve. Therefore, create the map in a way that makes it easy to modify. We recommend setting aside a weekend for the map-making, including breaks and individual reflection time. Consider it your 'offsite meeting' as the leadership team of your ICC.

From this point onward, we'll take you through the steps of completing the ICC Future Map, using our tools and advice. Once your map is finished, it's essential to look at all the items on it again. A reality check may make you decide to adapt or improve your Shared Vision, the strategic direction for getting there, or both.

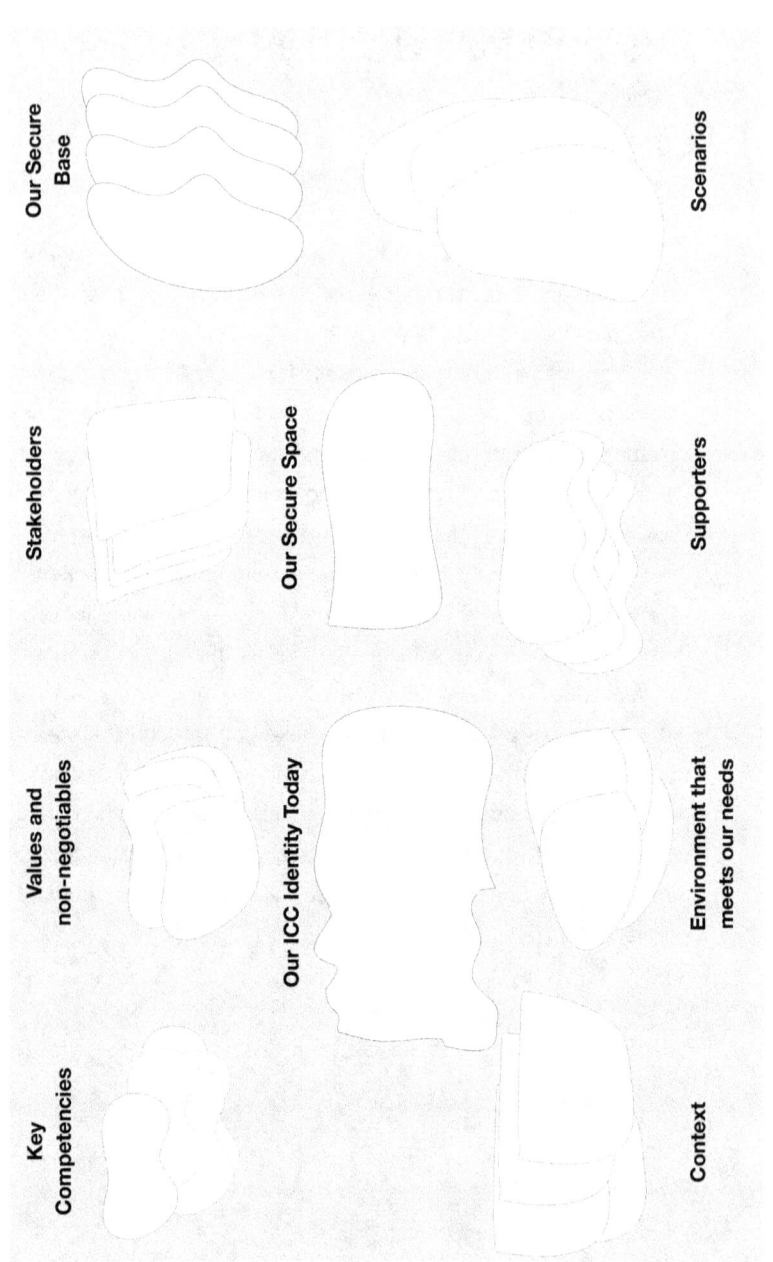

Mapping your Future as ICC template

Here are the various items to work through in order to build your Future Map:

- *Key Competencies* — your most important knowledge, skills, behaviours
- *Origins* — the individual identities that you both bring to the ICC (younger couples) / your starting point as an ICC
- *Context* – the current environment in which you're living and working (such as market constraints and opportunities, personal constraints, mobility)
- *Values and Non-Negotiables* — what you need to thrive as an ICC and what moves with you from location to location and from job to job
- *Environment That Meets Our Needs* — the organisational cultures and (local) circumstances that make you successful
- *Our ICC Identity* — who you are today as an ICC and how you present yourselves to your social and professional environments; your brand
- *Our Stakeholders* — the groups and individuals you must engage, in order to thrive as an ICC
- *Our Secure Bases* — relationships, belief systems and intangible inspirations that support and maintain you as individuals and as a couple, wherever you are
- *Our Secure Space* — where and when to have important conversations to envision, plan and decide on the future
- *Scenarios* — two or three career and lifestyle options you'll pursue to move you toward your Shared Vision (with the aim of realising one, or a combination, fully)
- *Shared Vision* — what you want to achieve over time as an ICC

Creating Your ICC Vision

We'll start at the righthand side of the map, where you ultimately want to end up—the Shared Vision—and then move on to the components that lead up to it. Why in that order? Well, your competencies, stakeholders, motivation and determination are of use only if they help you get where you want to go. In short, set the direction, and then plan how to get there. And remember, your Shared Vision is either a particular state you aim to achieve in the long term or the fulfilment of a purpose that guides you all along.

Here are three different methods you could use to develop your Shared Vision. Choose one that will suit you as a couple (it works best if you both use the same method). We recommend selecting the one you feel least familiar with, to stimulate your creativity. This exercise should take about 60 minutes to complete. In any case, make sure that you:

1. First, take time to think, individually, about where you want to go and what you want to achieve as independent people *and* as a couple.
2. Then sit together and share your results.
3. Finally, help each other to stimulate your ambitions.

This is not the moment to discuss what's realistic or not, nor to get bogged down in enumerating obstacles. Think big, think creatively, and map out a bright future for yourself!

Visioning method 1: questions to structure your thinking

This method allows you to establish a Shared Vision by using your rational thinking:

1. Individually, answer these questions one at a time:
   a. Where do you want to end up in five to ten years?
   b. What principle do you want to live by, always, in your partnership?
   c. What do you want to have achieved, as a couple and as individuals, later in life?
2. Discuss the individual answers together as a couple.
3. Then proceed to articulate your Shared Vision.

Visioning method 2: drawing to visualise your thinking

This method allows you to establish a Shared Vision by starting from your feelings:

1. Individually, take a piece of paper and draw a picture where you see yourself as a couple five to ten years from now.
   a. Don't use words or numbers, just images. You may want to use different colours.
   b. Show the pictures to each other afterwards. Listen first; then ask clarifying questions.
2. Then proceed to articulate your Shared Vision.

Once you've agreed on a Shared Vision, write it down on your map of the future.

Visioning method 3: artistic expressions to inspire your thinking

This method allows you to establish a Shared Vision by discovering your inspirations:

1. Individually, think of a piece of art that has left a big impression on you: a painting, sculpture, film, play, book, poem, or piece of music. Alternatively, walk around in a local art museum, and pick the object that attracts you most.
    a. What does this piece of art tell you about your self? What inspires you? What is really important to you?
    b. What does this artistic work tell you about your couple five to ten years from now? Can you describ this in words or images?
    c. Show and explain your choice to each other. Listen first; then ask clarifying questions.
2. Then proceed to articulate your Shared Vision.

"We've dreamed of perhaps doing something together one time, like building a business. We're looking for a stimulating environment to meet people with a story."

Antonella & Sergio

"Ever since Thomas and I met, we've wanted to create a place together. A unique conference centre, camping site, or any kind of place to gather globally-minded, creative spirits around good food, personal and professional development, in a beautiful natural setting. Looking at our choices up to now, we're gathering experience and stories to move us toward this vision. Let's see when we get there!"

Jannie [author]

STRATEGY: SCENARIO PLANNING

Now we proceed with the next step of Mapping Your Future. To arrive at a Shared Vision, your ICC needs a strategic direction, best expressed in scenarios. A scenario is a possible outcome for your couple, with the steps that lead to it.

ICCs often encounter unexpected opportunities and changing circumstances, so it's wise to choose from more than one scenario. Having options can allow you to fulfil your purpose more quickly, by (for example) going around a roadblock rather than removing it. (Some roadblocks—such as the need to care for elderly parents, limiting your mobility; or a market downturn that reduces career opportunities in one partner's industry—are difficult to be removed.) Given that an excessive number of scenarios may make you lose direction, we recommend developing at least two scenarios, but not more than four.

John & Martin's scenario planning

John and Martin needed to develop a scenario that had only one demanding job in the couple at a time, so that the other partner, while still involved in his career, could focus on the children. At the time of the interview, the couple was working together to grow John's healthcare business in Australia. Martin is expected to transition out of the company, once it is fully established. In about 10 years, another move may be on the horizon. The timing also depends on the need to care for John's elderly parents.

Antonella & Sergio's scenario planning

As a young couple, Antonella and Sergio are, as they call it, 'taking a sprint': working hard and progressing fast during the first five years. After that, they expect to settle down somehow. Another possible scenario for them is to move to a developing country in two to three years.

Three Important Conversations to Develop Scenarios

Developing your scenarios best happens through three conversations, each of which addresses one of the three elements that make up the ICC:

- The International Conversation
- The Career Conversation
- The Couple Conversation

Each conversation revolves around relevant questions. Each partner answers those questions first for himself or herself. Then, as a couple, you discuss the answers in order to find common ground. Based on the outcome of the three conversations, you then develop scenarios. Allow 30 minutes for each of the conversations and another 30 minutes for constructing the scenarios, so 120 minutes or two hours in total.

We list below a series of critical questions to guide you through each of the three conversations. The questions are meant to help you develop as many suitable options as possible, while limiting the options to those that will make you happy and successful. But before you get to the questions, here's a description of the overall conversation process:

1. Collect the data that will inform your three conversations, by having each partner individually answer the list of questions for each conversation (see below).

2. Then have each conversation, by discussing your individual answers together and finding common ground.
3. After completing the three conversations, construct two to four scenarios that you could pursue in the next five to ten years to achieve your Shared Vision.

Note: You need not have a specific answer to each and every question. If, for example, you don't have a preference for a type of location, then 'no preference' is your answer.

1. The International Conversation

This conversation is about establishing each partner's international mobility, any boundaries that may limit it, and the importance of international mobility for the careers and lives of the partners. Here are the questions (with sample categories of answers):

- *How mobile do I want to be?* (number of moves, locations, countries)
- *What do I see as my local environment?* (developed country, developing country, other particulars)
- *What is my international ambition?* (become a global citizen, expatriate)
- *What is my view on international lifestyle?* (urban, rural, international environment with lots of expats, 'hardship' posting, family-friendly)
- *What do I want to develop or learn?* (new language, intercultural leadership, preparing for a senior role in my organisation, fieldwork)
- *What type of local culture suits me best?* (similar to my home country, very different from my home country, international)

2. The Career Conversation

This conversation is about getting clarity on the professional ambitions and motivations of the partners. Here are the questions (with sample categories of answers):

- *What is the professional direction I want to take?* (marketing, general management, entrepreneur)
- *What do I see as my professional environment?* (NGO, FMCG, university)
- *What is my professional ambition?* (CFO, professor)
- *What's my view on work-life balance?* (maximum 1-hour commute, 4-day work week)
- *What do I want to develop or learn?* (MBA, Mandarin)
- *What type of organisational culture fits me best?* (up or out, team-based, informal)

3. The Couple Conversation

This conversation is about getting clarity on the partners' personal, couple-related and family ambitions and motivations, as well as on lifestyle choices. Here are the questions (with sample categories of answers):

- *What is the direction I want our couple to take?* (two-careers-no-kids, starting a family, setting the kids off to university, taking care of elderly parents)
- *What do I see as our couple/family environment?* (living in the same location, commuting between different locations)
- *What is my ambition for our couple?* (mutually support each other with our individual careers, or with alternate careers)
- *What's my view on role distribution within the couple?* (sharing the work, outsourcing to domestic staff)
- *What do I want to develop or learn?* (become a capable and loving working parent, developing an active social life)
- *What type of couple culture suits me best?* (family values, independent social lives).

"To experience Antonella with a clear career path inspired me to have the same. I saw an example to follow. It motivated me."

Sergio

MAPPING YOUR FUTURE AS ICC
Kashaf & Zaroon's Vision and Scenarios

Retirement without needing support from children.
Children become global citizens.

Our Secure Base

Stay abroad for next 10 years

Career opportunities for Kashaf in HR for the next 5-10 years

Zaroon progresses with current employer

Scenarios

Stakeholders

Our Secure Space

Supporters

Values and non-negotiables

Our ICC Identity Today

Environment that meets our needs

Key Competencies

Context

© Paul Vanderbroeck / Jannie Aasted Skov-Hansen

Origins : individual identities / starting point as ICC

KEY TAKEAWAYS FROM CHAPTER 3

Bravo! Well done! You've established your long-term direction as a couple and possible scenarios to get you there. Make sure you put them on your ICC Future Map. The subsequent chapters will help you fill in the rest of the map. But first here's a summary of what we've covered thus far on vision and success strategies:

Mapping Your Future is key to sustaining a successful ICC.

Start with developing a Shared Vision for your ICC.

A Shared Vision is either a particular state you aim to achieve in the long term, or the fulfilment of a purpose that guides you throughout your life.

Review your Shared Vision at regular intervals, but at least after every significant event or move.

Develop between two and four scenarios that give you strategic direction toward the Shared Vision.

Have three essential conversations to develop the scenarios: the International Conversation, the Career Conversation, and the Couple Conversation .

Adapt your scenarios as your ICC develops and the context around you evolves.

YOUR NOTES

Chapter 3 | *Here we are going*

CHAPTER 4

HERE WE ARE BECOMING: THE IDENTITY OF THE INTERNATIONAL CAREER COUPLE

WHAT IS AN ICC IDENTITY?

The need to choose and shape an identity distinguishes an ICC from a dual-career couple who stays in one country. That's not to say, of course, that moving within a country is free of challenges, but moving abroad is at a whole other level.

When moving abroad, an ICC confronts a different value system, perhaps a new language, and how locals perceive them. Where is 'home'? Is it somewhere existing and static? Or is your definition of home dynamic and evolving? You must assess, how those answers affect your identity as a couple and as a family. Couples who cross borders multiple times must develop an identity — a sense of their 'roots' — that sustains them and the family, independently of their location at a given time.

This chapter helps ICCs explore who they are, who they want to become, and how they want to be seen — during and after an international move.

How the ICC Identity is Distinct

The ICCs we interviewed see themselves as quite different from dual-career couples who are not internationally mobile. ICCs often have such couples in their networks, either at home or in their current location. And ICCs perceive the risks they face to be more significant than what domestic couples encounter. Still, they also know that their choices and opportunities are more extensive. For example, our ICCs perceived standard dual-career couples as having weekends full of local social commitments and as being less dependent on each other as partners.

"Given its greater complexity, an ICC has to deal with more variables, making it challenging to sustain the couple. Or it poses a risk of making you unhappy. Therefore, when you face a tough moment, it's harder to narrow down which variable is causing the problem. At the same time, complexity offers more opportunities. You build up other interests. It becomes more apparent what's essential in life, which is possible only when you're taken out of your setting. It allows you to reset, particularly regarding things you were not happy with in the past."

Martin

"It's now about 'the four of us in the world'. As a result, the dynamics of our family changed. We have fewer social obligations now. Weekends are empty. The boys are closer to each other. We're closer as a family. We develop new narratives. Everything is a bit edgy — not risky but edgy. The stakes are different, a bit more extreme. "

Silje

As an ICC, you'll always differ from the norm, both socially and professionally. Perhaps you'll find yourself in a large metropolitan and economically booming area, such as London or Singapore, and work and live around other dual-career couples. But because many of those couples will be permanently tied to the locality, they will have chosen a different lifestyle. Given your 'minority' identity, you must confront questions like:

- To what extent do we want to conform, and to remain different?
- Can our differences be an asset vis-à-vis the majority? If so, how?
- How do we present ourselves in our social and professional environments?
- And most important, do we feel okay with who we are and how we live?

WHY IDENTITY MATTERS FOR AN ICC

Working people have a social identity and a professional identity that, to an extent, overlap and mutually influence each other. The identities cannot be fully separated, as Harvard scholar Lakshmi Ramarajan makes clear in "Shattering the myth of separate worlds".

You may have a clearly defined role at work, but when you enter the office, you cannot leave your private self on the doorstep. For people pursuing a career, the overlap between the two identities is more extensive, because career is such a strong influencer of personal identity. Indeed, professional success depends on how much of the individual's self is put into the professional identity (that's why 'authenticity' is emphasised as a condition for leadership success). An ICC's identity is influenced by both partners' professional identities, with the additional factor of the international mobility that's tied to the career of at least one partner.

Humans dislike dealing with people they cannot identify. They want others to have a name and place in their context. That's why we ask get-to-know-you questions like "Where do you come from?" and "What do you do?". Such questions can sometimes lead to stereotyping and even discrimination, but they also help people build relationships and trust. People use this information to reduce the unknowns and adapt their behaviour in interactions with fellow human beings. Unknowns, as we've learned during thousands of years of evolution, can bring danger. People, after all, want to feel secure in their relationships. And there's not much we can do about that.

What ICCs can—and should—influence, however, is how their identities are constructed, whether actively (making or choosing the identity yourself) or passively (letting the identity be constructed by others). Constructing and communicating an identity determines how other people behave toward the ICC. What's more, a self-constructed identity based on being different and unique can make you more successful.

John & Martin's ICC Identity

Even before moving abroad, John and Martin noticed that they break many stereotypes in their social and professional lives. The combination of two professionally successful gay men from different countries with two children and no distinct roles in their couple, plus several international moves on their record, is rather distinctive. They have very busy social and professional lives, and they find it beneficial to show and emphasise particular parts of their identity in specific environments. So, for example, in a formal setting related to John's work as the CEO of his company (where Martin is currently the COO), they make it less evident to others that they are in an equal partnership.

Silje & Tim's ICC Identity

Even before moving, Silje and Tim consciously constructed an identity as an ICC. Singapore has many expatriates, 90% of whom are men. Silje and Tim purposely present themselves as a career couple in social settings. It's equally important for them to be transparent that Silje is the expat and Tim the locally employed spouse.

In career development, the phenomenon of developing and using an identity is called 'branding'. A brand is the relationship between how a professional is perceived and their employability. Most career coaches advise actively managing your brand to develop a career, rather than letting the external environment determine the brand. As an ICC, you'll be subject to stereotypes, and not necessarily positive ones. For example, if your partner is pursuing his or her own career, rather than taking care of things at home, future employers may think that your family could cause you trouble at work, or that your partner's job may reduce your international mobility.

Actually, when it comes to identity, ICCs hold an advantage over other dual-career couples and single-career couples. Hajo Adam from Rice University ("The shortest path to oneself leads around the world") shows that the longer you move abroad, the better you know yourself. In this complex and volatile world, everybody struggles to find their place. Thanks to their international experience, ICC partners get to know themselves better as individuals and as a couple. Abroad, you continuously have the chance to confront and benchmark your personal and cultural values, norms, and behaviours against a foreign culture. The resulting self-reflection generates a more transparent concept of self, helping the partners to construct an ICC identity that truly fits them. The more you know yourself, the clearer your identity is, and the better your choices (for instance, regarding a career move) are.

In his book *Leadership Strategies for Women*, Paul Vanderbroeck [author] has shown leveraging difference to be a critical success factor for women leaders. Such tactics also work for ICCs, who similarly find themselves outside the norm. It's not about fighting stereotypes, but disarming them or turning them to your advantage.

For example, being a career spouse, rather than a stay-at-home spouse, makes it initially more difficult to get things organised at home in a new location. Nonetheless, such a spouse can be a trusted adviser and coach. Yes, a career spouse makes international mobility more challenging—but once successfully relocated, a career spouse is more likely to ensure the success of the expatriation than an unhappy stay-at-home spouse is. These can be compelling arguments in a career discussion with a boss. Plus, feeling okay about who you are and who you're becoming boosts your confidence and binds the couple together.

FINDING AND BUILDING AN ICC IDENTITY

Forming an Identity: Antonella & Sergio

Antonella and Sergio left their home country a few years ago. Soon they noticed that their social network in the new location was quite different from the friends they left behind and stay in touch with. Their new friends are mostly in the same situation: ambitious professionals from different countries. Antonella and Sergio find the amiable competition among the couples to be stimulating. And the social group has a healthy routine of celebrating their friends' professional successes.

Forming an Identity: Kashaf & Zaroon

Even before moving abroad, being different was part of the DNA of Kashaf and Zaroon's partnership. They grew up in opposite parts of the country, which are culturally very distinct. Their love was able to bridge the divide. Therefore, back home, they were already considered a role-model couple in their community.

Identity, as mentioned before, gives a name and a place to where a person belongs. Being rooted in one location and working for a single employer make it easier to construct an identity that offers a sense of belonging. But where do you belong if you move across borders? How do you avoid feeling isolated?

To address these questions, we adapted our advice from recent research on the identities of individuals pursuing a career—for instance, by Gianpiero Petriglieri (yes, Jennifer's husband) in "Crafting portable selves for contemporary careers". Gianpiero argues that because lifetime employment with a single organisation is no longer the norm, developing a career across different organisations demands a 'portable' self.

ICCs, too, need a portable identity to move among countries, even if one or both partners continue to work for the same employer. A mobile identity prevents the feeling of rootlessness and responds to the need to belong. It's independent of your location and therefore empowering.

Expressing Identity: John & Martin

Every year John and Martin send a funny Christmas card to their friends and family all over the world. It shows a picture in which they dress up in amusing costumes as a family.

Other ICCs we interviewed mentioned the identity of 'global citizens', which they often first notice in their children.

Identity Categories

It's possible to distinguish between two categories of portable individual identities: externally and internally anchored:

- For ICCs, an *externally anchored* identity is one defined in terms of a broad social identity (such as 'expatriate' or one's employer, for example, Unilever or the United Nations).
- An *internally anchored* identity draws from values one holds dear or one's authentic self—for example, 'making people better' or 'wealth creation'.

ICC identities are, by definition, unique, so we want to be prudent not to put people in boxes. The broad categories can nevertheless help you construct your identity as ICC.

ICCs with an externally anchored identity often are permanent or frequent expatriates, assigned to different countries by an employer. Most of their lives and careers happen outside their home country in an international professional and personal environment. They are the couples whose children attend international schools, even during stints in the home country, because the family moves every few years to another nation. Typical examples: a couple with one or two partners who are diplomats; a long-term careerist in a multinational company.

Externally Anchored ICC Identity: Kashaf & Zaroon

Kashaf and Zaroon thus far have been working outside their home country, having been expatriated twice by Karim's NGO employer. They intend to continue in this way for the foreseeable future. Working for the same employer offers an external anchor. So does their active membership in their community of faith, regardless of the family's location.

ICCs with an internally anchored identity move across borders, often at their initiative and several times during their lifetime. The opportunities and experience offered by a new country allow them to fulfil their aspirations or do work that aligns with their values. Examples: couples who seek out new cultures and new experiences, or who wish to offer humanitarian aid wherever it's needed.

Internally Anchored ICC Identity: Antonella & Sergio

Antonella and Sergio's identity is anchored in finding opportunities to do research they're passionate about.

In our own research, we also found ICCs who have a combined internal and external anchor.

Internally and Externally Anchored ICC Identity: Silje & Tim

Silje and Tim are externally anchored to Silje's employer, who initiated their expatriation. At the same time, the couple is internally anchored to their strong desire to stay (financially) independent from an employer—or, say, a house—in a specific location.

In the end, for an ICC, it doesn't matter whether you're internally or externally anchored, or both. But having an anchor that provides stability in mobility does matter. You need something to hold onto throughout the changes and instability that inevitably come with an internationally mobile life and career. Identity anchoring is closely connected to having a secure base, which we'll discuss in *Chapter 5 — Here We Change:* People who offer stability through change provide such a base. The anchor is its non-human equivalent.

As an ICC has more experiences, its identity changes as well as becomes more distinct. Meaningful experiences are retold in the form of stories.

Building an Identity Through Stories: Silje & Tim

Silje and Tim recommend each ICC to build their personal narrative of their life through stories like: *Remember the time in Asia when our son Rasmus did...?*

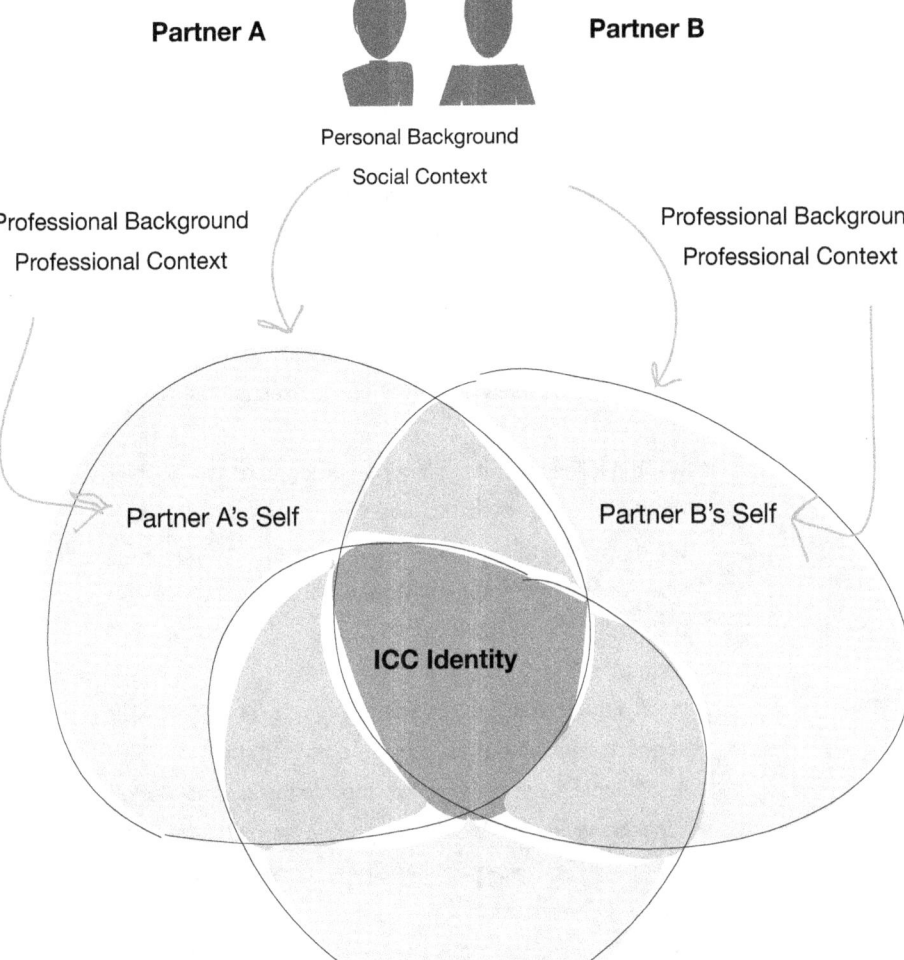

Chapter 4 | *Here we are becoming*

ICC Identity Exercise

Now it's time to work on your own identity. We recommend doing the following exercise before or after each relocation, in addition to including it in your Mapping the Future as ICC. Relocation requires a rebuilding of individual identities, unless the professional identities of both partners are already portable. The ICC identity shifts as a result: As intercultural trainer Kathy Borys Siddiqui puts it, "An international identity is continuously evolving and resembles a muscle—we are the ones able to build and shape it."

Allow 45 to 60 minutes to go through the exercise, as follows:

1. Answer the following questions alone or together as a couple:
    - What key characteristics identify me as a person, a professional and a partner?
    - How do the different individual identities that are the building blocks of our identity as an ICC complement each other?
    - What key characteristics identify us as an ICC in our social and professional environments?
    - As a couple, what image do we show to the external world?
    - What behaviour do we display that is typical of the identity of our ICC? How would external parties recognise us as the ICC we are?
    - As individuals, how do we express our ICC's identity at the workplace?
    - Where are we anchored as an ICC? Are we more internally or externally anchored? Or do we, perhaps, have two anchors?
    - What stories do we share, as a couple or a family, that are the foundations of our identity?
    - Based on all of these questions, what are the key characteristics of our ICC?

1. Discuss the individual answers together as a couple.
2. Then proceed to develop an identity for you as an ICC. Who are we as an ICC?
3. How do we help our children embrace, understand and express the identity of our ICC?
    - How will we express our ICC's identity at our respective workplaces?
    - How will we express our ICC's identity in our social environment?
    - You can express the identity in the form of an introduction or an elevator speech: "Hi, I am..., the spouse of...who is.., and together we are...."

Well done! Now you have additional information to insert on your Future Map—specifically, your ICC identity and your starting point (your origins as a couple).

Your Origins as a Couple

Take 10 minutes to list the origins of your couple on the left side of the map. For couples together less than five years, we recommend listing individual origins. Our survey of ICCs suggests that personal origins affect ICCs more significantly at this earlier stage of a relationship.

For more established ICCs, like Kashaf and Zaroon, it's more relevant to talk about where you're coming from as a couple. Here is Kashaf and Zaroon's map, now with the information about origins and ICC identity:

MAPPING YOUR FUTURE AS ICC
Kashaf & Zaroon's Identity and Origins

Vision: Retirement without needing support from children
Children become global citizens

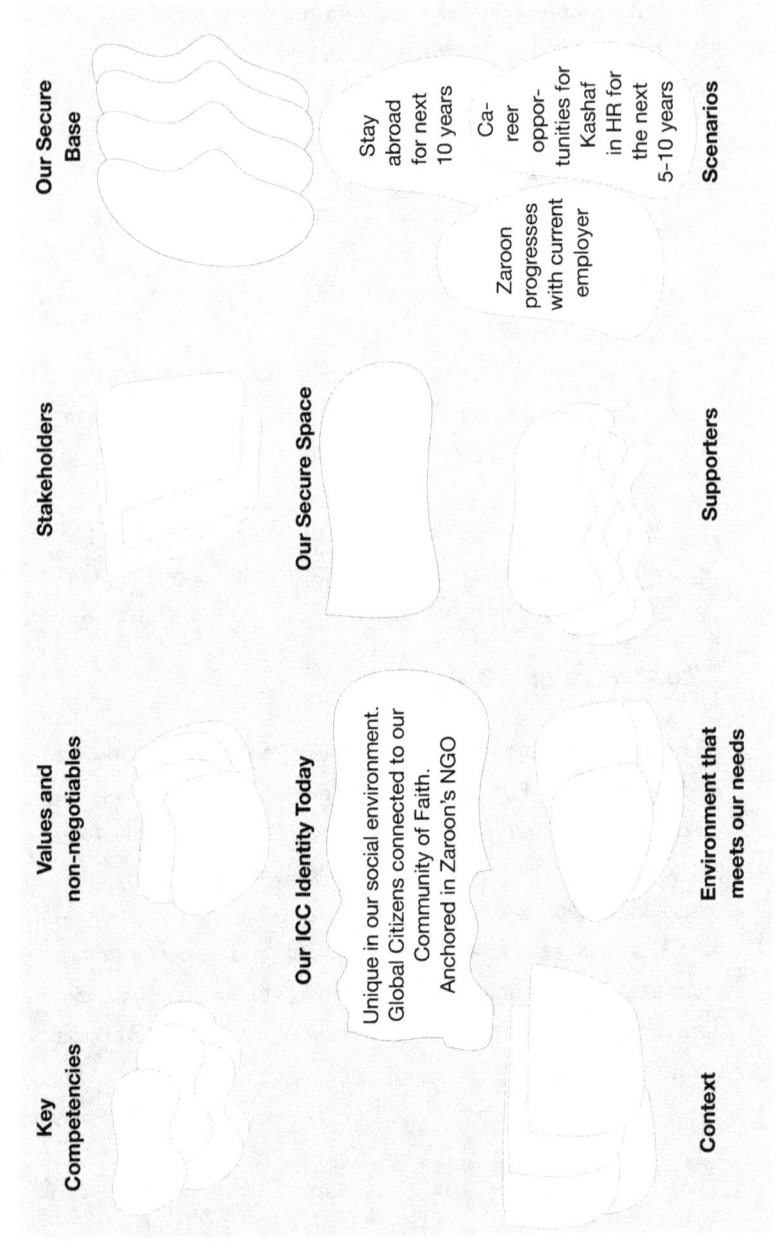

Origins: South Asia; Community of Faith,
different from others in home country

© Paul Vanderbroeck / Jannie Aasted Skov-Hansen

KEY TAKEAWAYS FROM CHAPTER 4

CCs need to develop a mobile identity that sustains the couple and the family over time. This identity prevents the feeling of rootlessness and responds to the need to belong. It is independent of geographical location and therefore empowering.

Feeling okay about who they are and who they're becoming boosts the confidence of both partners—and binds the couple together.

By actively constructing and communicating an identity, ICCs can influence how others interact with the couple and the individual partners.

CC identity — as a brand — particularly if based on uniqueness, is helpful for the career development of the partners.

YOUR NOTES

CHAPTER 5

HERE WE CHANGE: SUSTAINING THE INTERNATIONAL CAREER COUPLE OVER TIME

Life and career events require ICCs to adapt their strategy and how they implement it over time. As David Campbell wrote in *If You Don't Know Where You're Going, You'll Probably End Up Somewhere Else,* "Practically all goals tarnish with time if not renewed in some way." Indeed, change is a central leadership challenge for ICCs.

Earlier, we heard Martin explain how many more variables ICCs must juggle, compared with other dual-career couples. How true! It's the same when it comes to change. Because of international mobility, the changes ICCs face are especially complex and significantly affect everything private and professional for the couple. This complexity infuses both the self-initiated and the unplanned changes that life and careers bring.

Best practices in change leadership that make organisations successful and sustainable also can help ICCs thrive. You may already be familiar with these ideas from your workplace, such as John Kotter's advice on leading change. No need to repeat it here. Instead, let's identify some concepts and best practices that our research has shown to be particularly relevant to ICCs.

Chapter 3 explained how to develop a Shared Vision. Now we'll cover the two other critical success factors for ICCs: Secure Space, a process that helps an ICC to plan for change and make critical decisions effectively; and Mutual Career Development, which is part of a larger change leadership practice to manage risks and opportunities on an ongoing basis.

SECURE SPACE

Our research shows that ICCs benefit from creating a Secure Space where they comfortably make strategic decisions about career moves, relocation, financial investments, and so on. In this space, the partners share and refine their thoughts and feelings about events at work or home. It can be a physical space (kitchen, bedroom, favourite restaurant) or a virtual space ('date night'). Often the Secure Space takes the form of a ritual that helps to focus the mind on key decisions and segregate these moments from day-to-day tasks. Having the space helps to sustain the ICC over time, by keeping you on track toward your Shared Vision or adapting the vision if needed.

Joëlle and Paul [author], for example, have a Secure Space of smoking a cigar together on their balcony. (They picked up this vice during a trip to Cuba, early in their relationship.) In this space, the couple has a safe context for figuring out things that matter. In *Chapter 6 – Here We Are Getting There*, we'll discuss how to have such important conversations.

Silje & Tim's Secure Space

"We do talk a lot. We are in constant conversation, often while taking a walk in the evening or when we can share a ride on the train to work. We tend to find small moments, small pockets—and integrate those into the day."

"We plan a lot. Therefore, we have less stress. We drink chai at night when the kids are sleeping. So before moving to Kyrgyzstan, we researched the place, browsed the internet, and set up appointments before we arrived. We were uncomfortable going where there was no place of worship or community centre for our community of faith. So, at first, we refused. Then we developed scenarios of what it could be like. After one year, we said yes. Now we're happy to be here."

Kashaf & Zaroon

John & Martin's Secure Space

John and Martin have their crucial conversations in the evening in their living room, when the kids are in bed. When they disagree, both nevertheless commit to the decision taken. The important thing is that both of their viewpoints have been heard. As a result, they rarely go back on a decision.

Secure Space Exercise

Before adding the next piece to your Future Map, we suggest reflecting on which Secure Space you're using or how you can develop one. Allow 30 minutes for this exercise. Sit together with a notebook or some paper available. Reflect on and discuss the following points:

1. Where, when and how do we have discussions about important matters concerning our future as a couple?
2. Does this space allow us to have a confidential, uninterrupted conversation?
3. Do we have a ritual that makes these moments special and sets them apart from other discussions and time together?
4. Do we want to keep it this way? If not, how can we improve it?
5. If needed, take some time to brainstorm possibilities.
6. Decide on the way forward.
7. Note your Secure Space on your ICC Future Map.

SECURE BASE AND MUTUAL CAREER DEVELOPMENT

Change is inherently connected to risk and opportunity. Few people are daredevils when it comes to their lives and careers. That's particularly so for ICCs because of how much is at stake: a life partnership, two careers, financial assets and commitments, often a family.

Change is unavoidable when moving across borders, when developing careers and while the couple matures. It makes sense to embark on such an adventure while someone or something has your back. George Kohlrieser and Susan Goldsworthy, from IMD Business School, developed for organisations what they call a 'secure base', defined as "a person, place, goal or object that provides a sense of protection, safety and caring and offers a source of inspiration and energy for daring, exploration, risk-taking and seeking challenge."

For ICCs, our research has led us to expand the definition to include: "A trusted relationship with individuals that both stretch and challenge you and provide care and support."

Jennifer Petriglieri uses the concept as well. She claims that providing a secure base to each other is vital for dual-career couples—more so when it's symmetrical, such that the partners are each other's secure base. When the dynamic goes both ways, it deepens the couple's relationship while stimulating both partners to grow professionally. Secure bases are essential to ICCs, as they are to any dual-career couple. Antonella and Sergio, our youngest couple, provide an example.

By providing a secure base, leaders can apply the concept

"Our closest support network is each other."

Antonella & Sergio

of 'care to dare', which means releasing followers from fears that get in the way of their performance. The concept is particularly useful for leading change in organisations, as we have learned from Susan Goldsworthy. We believe that it is also helpful for leading change in the ICC, notably regarding Mutual Career Development. In the ICC, the partners apply shared leadership which also means that the partners sometimes alternate between the role of leader and follower. In the illustration below, we've adapted the care to dare concept for Mutual Career Development in the ICC.

Mutual Career Development in International Career Couples

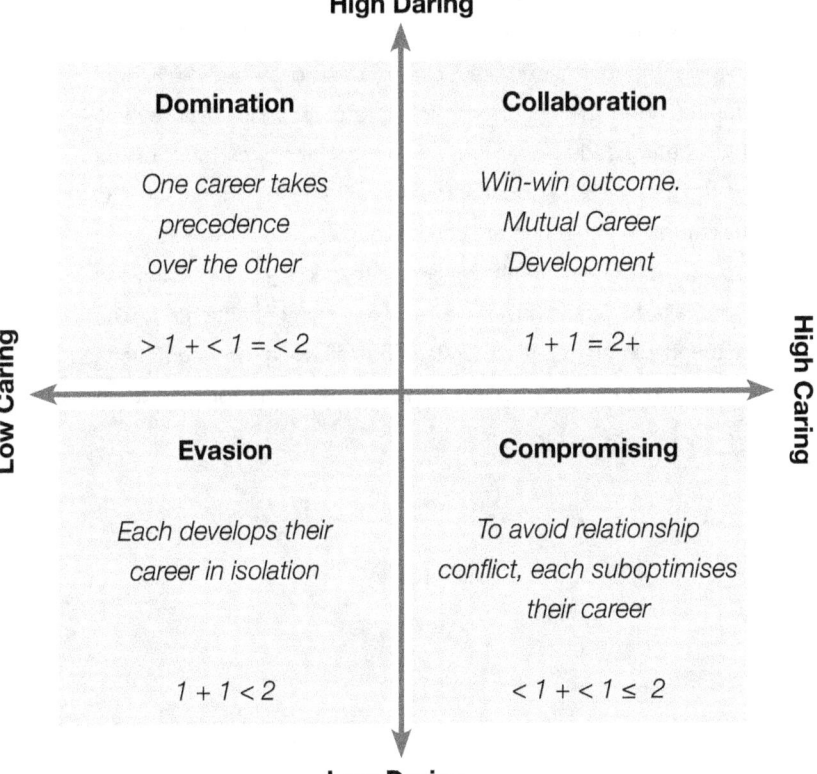

Ref: Adapted Kohlrieser, Goldsworthy & Coombe

Mutual Career Development in International Career Couples

For an ICC, collaboration is essential for any positive change, both the 'dare' of taking risks and the 'care' of nurturing the couple. Only then can an ICC add constant value to the couple and both partners' careers.

Perfect balance is not always necessary, though. Often, one partner is more daring while the other is more caring at certain junctures. As explained in Chapter 2, on Mutual Career Development – a critical success factor –, sometimes one partner gets help from the other; at other times, the roles are reversed. Of the successful ICCs we surveyed, 70% feel 'Highly responsible' for the career success of their partner, almost all involve the partner in key career decisions, and 90% feel support from their partner in job and career. However, overall balance is needed over time. If one partner does most of the caring and the other most of the daring for long periods, the ICC risks turning into a primary career couple.

It took seven months for Sergio to land a job after following Antonella to Scandinavia. He received many rejections. It was a tough period for his morale. The following two quotations from Sergio and Antonella capture the back-and-forth between caring and daring:

"When Sergio followed me to Scandinavia, I felt anxious. How to find a solution that worked for both of us? Then to see Sergio's success in finding a career opportunity was a high point in our relationship. He impressed me, and at the same time, I felt relieved."

Antonella

"Antonella had an extensive network that helped and gave advice. It was encouraging to see other people who had managed to enter the local job market. It motivated me to continue to apply for positions. To follow Antonella was the best choice of my life."

Sergio

Here are some potential pitfalls with caring and daring:

- Too much daring and too little caring generally imply valuing career over couple. It may work to develop two successful international careers, but at the expense of well-being within the couple.
- Too much caring and too little daring may occur in ICCs who evolve into a local dual-career couple because they consider moving abroad to be too risky.
- When there is little caring *and* little daring, the partners are afraid to put their desires and ambitions on the table. Or they're not seeking to understand such feelings and wishes in their partner. This dynamic makes it impossible to develop a vision and strategy for the long-term success of the couple.

Having a secure base prepares you for the risk that opens the door to opportunities. It provides a source of resilience. It helps the ICC bounce back from setbacks and hardships.

Our research tells us that sources of security outside the couple also can be beneficial. These sources may be groups, such as the couple's extended families, or a close-knit and strongly delimited professional group, such as the medical profession or academic researchers. Security also may stem from a belief system, grounded in faith, philosophy, arts and literature.

We therefore recommend that ICCs identify and develop an external secure base in addition to providing a secure base to each other. John and Martin, for instance, believe that their secure base is rooted in the strong values they share. Kashaf and Zaroon rely on their faith.

"A shared value throughout our marriage has been a global mindset and the joy of intercultural collaboration. From when we set out as development workers in rural Nepal to our current involvement in a corporate and political organisational setting, respectively, we have always strived to maximise our impact. We simply wish to help make the world a better place. This secure base has guided us in professional choices upon returning to Denmark as re-pats and continues to be the backbone of our professional lives."

Jannie [author]

John & Martin's Mutual Career Support

From the beginning, John and Martin have been alternating their careers. When moving from one country to another, they've switched roles between career focus and family focus. Relocating back to Australia from Europe, it was John's turn to focus on his career. He wanted to set up his own healthcare company. They decided to make a significant investment in a building, but only after Martin managed to impose that they develop a business plan, using his skills as a management consultant. It was a big change for Martin to go independent and become a business owner. It was easier for John, who intuitively knew there was a market. John's entrepreneurial spirit met and clashed with Martin's organised business-planning perspective. It eventually worked as a combination of strong shared values, gut feeling, and planning.

> "When the opportunity to move to Singapore came up, we talked. We came quickly to a positive decision. Yet I was conscious of the need for Tim to have a job. I felt the pressure of responsibility for Tim and the realisation that I would have to spend a lot of time away in the new job."
>
> Silje

Silje & Tim's Mutual Career Support

Some five years ago, Tim was frustrated at work. This happens regularly with Tim. He underwent a tough period. Silje used her HR coaching skills to help him through these difficult times. On occasion, it has been helpful for Silje to ask Tim to stop complaining.

Silje had a challenging period once, too. She felt alone and frustrated. Tim helped her with important work assignments. He managed to get her back on the ground and used a structured approach to help her take action. From these experiences, they've learned to help each other professionally on an ongoing basis.

A couple needs a secure base that goes beyond Mutual Career Support. But the two careers are so essential to the ICC's success that Mutual Career Support forms the essence of its secure base.

Mutual Career Development Exercise

Now you can assess how you're doing in supporting each other's careers. Use the following exercise to identify and improve your Mutual Career Development and identify or develop your external secure base. Allow 45 minutes for this exercise:

1. Sit together, and take out a sheet of paper.
2. Draw an empty Mutual Career Development grid.
3. Write down some of the more recent behaviours you've engaged in to support each other's careers and professional situations. Also include things you haven't done, particularly for the bottom two boxes (Evasion and Compromising).
4. Discuss the outcomes.
5. Identify possible (individual) improvements to findmore behaviours that go in the top-right corner (Collaboration)—and list unhelpful behaviours in the other three boxes.
6. Commit to actions, and agree when you will discuss those actions in your Secure Space.
7. Identify what your external secure bases are or could be.
8. Note the external secure bases on your ICC Future Map.

STAKEHOLDERS

Change can mean different things. Often it requires changing roles in the couple and at work. With that comes a new identity, or a re-branding of yourself and perhaps—but not necessarily—your couple. Regardless, leading change successfully requires managing and influencing expectations from stakeholders, for change doesn't happen in a vacuum.

Stakeholders include individuals and groups who have an interest in the change you want to achieve as an ICC. Remember: all the people in your secure base are stakeholders, as they have a practical or an emotional stake in the ICC's success. Your spouse should be part of the secure base, but he or she is also a stakeholder, by definition. And, of course, beyond the secure base are more stakeholders, some of whom may not unequivocally support the ICC's goals. Part of leading change is to influence stakeholders and bring them along toward your Shared Vision.

Let's help you identify your most important stakeholders, their perspective on your vision, and how you can influence them so that you get maximum support. Broadly speaking, ICCs have two types of stakeholders:

1. Stakeholders who have power and can use it to either support or oppose the change.
2. Stakeholders who need support, which could consume resources required for the change.

Each stakeholder is more or less aligned toward the ICC's goals. The objectives in influencing the stakeholders are as follows:

1. **Stakeholders with power**
    a. Influence them toward more alignment, so that the stakeholders use their power for support
    b. Influence them toward neutralising the power if not aligned, so that their use of power becomes less obstructive

2. **Stakeholders who need support**
    a. Empower them, in order to reduce their need for support
    b. Shift resources toward delegation to save resources directly spent by the ICC.

John & Martin's stakeholders

John and Martin have synchronised their relocation (to start up John's business) with the need to care for John's elderly parents in Australia. To allow both partners to work full-time and spend quality time with their children, they use an au pair for daily childcare.

Kashaf & Zaroon's stakeholders

Kashaf and Zaroon have created a small community in Kyrgyzstan with private gatherings and readings for the families who belong to their faith. This change has accelerated their integration into the new location by providing a source of meaning and support, both privately and professionally.

ICC Stakeholder Mapping

You can map your stakeholders according to the types just described. It helps to identify an influencing strategy for each stakeholder. Here is an ICC Stakeholder Map with examples of stakeholders and influencing strategies (adapted from Peter Block, *The Empowered Manager*).

ICC Stakeholder Map :
Influencing Stakeholders with examples

Degree of Alignment with the ICC's Goals

High

Well-Wishers
e.g. Friends from Home
Empower

Allies
New Employer
Leverage

Potential Allies
e.g. Adolescent Children
Discover Potential

Show-Stoppers
e.g. Elderly Parents
Empathize
Delegation

Opposers
e.g. Current Employer
Make a Deal

Low

Low Power / Needs Support   *Needs / Can Give Support*   *High Power / Can Give Support*

Chapter 5 | *Here we change*   151

Legend of the Stakeholder Map:

- *Well-Wishers:* individuals or groups who strongly support your vision as an ICC. They, however, offer little concrete support. Your strategy is to increase their power. Well-wishers might be friends from your past in your home country. Can you find a way to empower them, so that their support becomes more tangible?
- *Show-Stoppers:* individuals or groups who depend on your support and who may fear that your plans get in the way of their needs. Your strategies are to reduce their need for support and to make them feel more positively about where you want to go. Possible show-stoppers are elderly parents in need of care. Showing empathy for their situation could make them more aligned with your goals. Can you give them support in a way that reduces the negative effect on your mobility?
- *Potential Allies:* individuals or groups who may depend on you in some areas while providing help in others. Their attitude toward your plans is neutral and could go either way. Your strategy is to influence these stakeholders toward more alignment and more support for you as an ICC. Potential allies, for example, are adolescent children. First, discover their potential. Then see how you can develop that potential toward less dependence and more support while also turning them into allies.
- *Allies:* individuals or groups who have a stake in your success as an ICC — but who also have power. This power may be access to resources, to give you support that helps you realise your goals. They may be able to do even more for you. Your strategy is to proactively leverage your allies' power. The new employer of a partner who wants them to relocate

to a different country is an obvious example. What can you ask for to make the transition more successful for your ICC?

- *Opposers:* individuals or groups with power who are negatively inclined toward your future as an ICC. Perhaps your plans clash with their interests. Your influencing strategy is to reduce the opposition, for example by entering into a negotiation to arrive at a win-win solution. An opposer could be the current employer of the partner, whose spouse has been offered an expatriation. A talented staff member who follows their partner abroad leaves a gap behind, which may be difficult to fill. This opposer could frustrate the ICC's opportunity. What deal can you strike, or what can you offer to mitigate the negative impact for this stakeholder?

Now you can create the Stakeholder Map for your ICC and develop your influencing strategy. Allow 45 minutes for this exercise:

1. Sit together, and take out a sheet of paper.
2. Draw an empty Stakeholder Map.
3. Identify your ICC stakeholders.
4. Position each stakeholder depending on their level of alignment with your goals, the amount of power they have, or the level of support they need or can give.
    a. Alignment: To what extent does the stakeholder agree with and support your goals as an ICC? Mostly, such alignment depends on what your goals—e.g., an international move—mean for the stakeholder. Do your goals bring advantages or disadvantages to the stakeholder? Do your goals in any way disagree with the stakeholder's values?
    b. Power and Support: Does the ICC in any way

depend on the support of the stakeholder? And how important is that support? Or is there a stakeholder that depends on the ICC for support? How much help can a stakeholder give?
5. Proceed with developing an influencing strategy for each stakeholder. The strategy should aim to maximise support and alignment from your stakeholders.
6. Depending on where the greatest urgency is—and the most significant opportunity for results—agree on your top three influencing strategies.
7. Then make an action plan: Who does what—and when?

Now that you've created your Stakeholder Map and influencing strategy, put the most important stakeholder(s) on your Future Map.

MAPPING YOUR FUTURE AS ICC
Kashaf & Zaroon's Map including leading change elements

Vision : Retirement without needing support from children
Children become global citizens

Our Secure Base
- Community of Faith
- Couple

Scenarios
- Stay abroad for next 10 years
- Career opportunities for Kashaf in HR for the next 5-10 years
- Zaroon progresses with current employer

Stakeholders
- Zaroon's employer
- Relatives back home

Our Secure Space
- Chai hour

Supporters

Values and non-negotiables

Our ICC Identity Today
Unique in our social environment. Global Citizens connected to our Community of Faith. Anchored in Zaroon's NGO

Environment that meets our needs

Key Competencies

Context

© Paul Vanderbroeck / Jannie Aasted Skov-Hansen

Origins : South Asia; Community of Faith, different from others in home country

Chapter 5 | *Here we change*   155

KEY TAKEAWAYS FROM CHAPTER 5

Good work! While going through the exercises, you've covered much ground with this chapter. Make sure you complete the relevant items in your Future Map.

Frequent change is a given for ICCs. Change leadership is required to master the ICC's challenges successfully.

Having a Secure Space is a critical success factor for an ICC. In this protected space or context, the couple freely and confidentially discusses things that matter. A ritual can help to facilitate such conversations.

Leading change is more likely to be successful from secure bases: relationships and people who provide support and challenges.

Mutual Career Support, a critical success factor for an ICC, forms the essence of its secure base.

Leading change requires influencing stakeholders in a variety of ways, so that an ICC gets maximum support.

YOUR NOTES

Chapter 5 | *Here we change*

CHAPTER 6

HERE WE ARE DEVELOPING: HUMAN RESOURCE MANAGEMENT IN THE INTERNATIONAL CAREER COUPLE

For an ICC to be successful and sustainable, its two leaders must manage its human resources. But of course, an ICC's human resources and its leaders are one in the same—the partners themselves. Below we cover the aspects of HR management that are strategically relevant to an ICC.

ICC KEY COMPETENCIES, VALUES, AND THE ENVIRONMENT YOU NEED

The principle that past success predicts future success is a proven one. With that in mind, you'll now begin a data-gathering exercise we call the 'ICC TimeLine'. The aim is to analyse the moments that have most significantly influenced your development as an ICC, both professionally and personally. The exercise will reveal some important constants that deserve to be leveraged, all in service of your ICC's success.

ICC TimeLine Exercise

Here's how to proceed (allow one hour in total for this exercise; the first 20 minutes on your own):

1. On your own (not with your partner), write down—in chronological order—the decisions, non-financial contributions, recognitions, awards, important changes, and so on that you consider to be 'defining positive moments' during your professional and private life as a couple. These are your 'highs'. (If you've been together less than five years, include some moments from before you became a couple.)
2. Then do the same for your 'lows'—defining moments that

you consider to have been setbacks, disappointments, and failures.
3. For each high and low, think back and write down:
   a. What did you, individually and as a couple, do that made this moment happen? Please also include things you avoided or didn't do that enabled this moment to become a high or a low.
   b. What were you feeling and thinking at the time?
   c. What contextual aspects contributed in a significant way to this moment's being a high or a low?
   d. Recall the feedback, related to these moments, that you received from stakeholders at work and in your personal life.
   e. Finally, try to identify patterns over time, in the following categories:
      i. Behaviours: What are your most essential competencies as an ICC that you often bring to bear to reach a successful outcome?
      ii. Thoughts and Feelings: What is really important to you (your values)? What is non-negotiable for you?
      iii. Context: What type of environment makes your ICC thrive?
4. Come together as a couple and draw a timeline, like the example below. (A flipchart, table, or wall with sticky notes works best.)
5. Plot your respective highs and lows chronologically on the timeline.
   a. See where the two of you overlap in your highs and lows.
   b. Share the results of your individual analyses, ask clarifying questions, and give each other feedback.

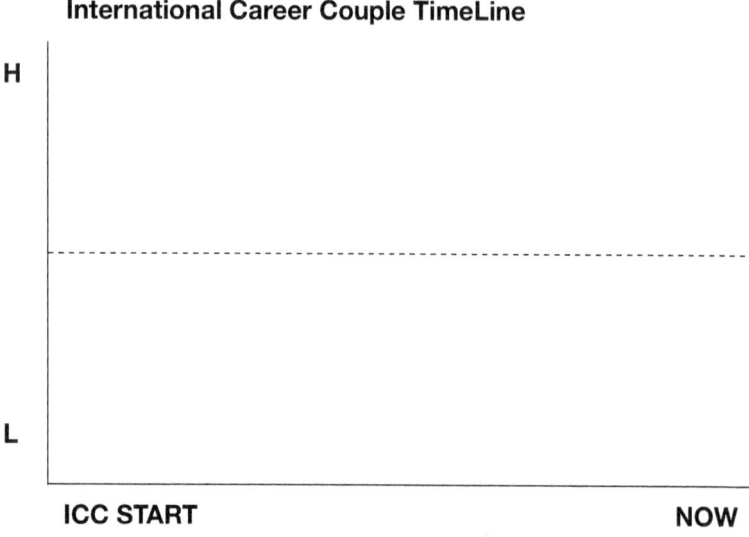

6. Now that you have a graphic representation of the respective milestones of your personal and professional history as a couple, it's time to agree on the following:
   a. What are the key competencies of and within your ICC that bring you success? We suggest agreeing on two to five competencies.
   b. What are your values as an ICC? Where do you draw a boundary—in other words, what is not negotiable?
   c. In what environment(s) does your ICC flourish, professionally and privately?

The following quotation shows how the two partners in an ICC became aware of their values during a defining moment:

> "Both of us come from families with a breadwinner. We've always wanted that for our children, that there's always one parent home for them. We're not comfortable with outsourcing their education. When Martin adopted John's children, we had to explain our values to the authorities. That forced us to think about them. Now we know that we can build a solid family without giving up any career."
>
> John & Martin

Examples from ICCs

Key competency
- Antonella and Sergio have become good at career development coaching, which increases their mobility. Apart from helping themselves, others now come to them for help and advice.
- Joëlle and Paul [author] have developed a competency to facilitate dinner parties that allow different and new people to interact socially and professionally. These activities accelerate their integration into a new environment.

Values / Non-negotiable
- Silje and Tim want to stay independent of employers or financial commitments.
- Quality schooling for their son is not negotiable for Joëlle and Paul [author].

Environment
- Kashaf and Zaroon need an environment that provides schooling for their children.
- Joëlle and Paul [author] thrive in an urban environment that offers lots of opportunities for intellectual and cultural stimulation.

"We believe that our experience moving to different countries—and, hence, finding solutions together to all the ensuing challenges over time—has made us a powerful team. It has given us a high level of trust in each other. Now we know that we can overcome any challenge together, because we support each other. And we've learned that our great level of communication and good stamina are two key competencies that have facilitated this progress."

Antonella & Sergio

After this exercise, add your conclusions to your Future Map.

INTERNATIONAL COMPETENCIES

Having discussed the team competencies of your ICC, you can turn to the competencies of the two individual partners. Individual competencies, particularly of talented people, change over time. Therefore, the HR management for the ICC must attend to the competency development of the partners. From our research, we know that such competencies are both professional and personal.

For an ICC, these competencies also have an international component. HERE WE ARE GLOBAL has developed a Competency Matrix for internationally mobile professionals. We'll use it here to help you develop individual competencies that are relevant to your ICC.

As you'll see, the Competency Matrix addresses several areas of life. We therefore use a holistic framework to depict how you, as a global professional, can choose to build and expand your skillset in an international setting. Our ambition is to inspire and help you visualise your 'visionary best' and, from there, identify and prioritise actions to develop the future 'you'.

The HERE WE ARE Competency Matrix® lets you explore how to design your trajectory and look at life from new perspectives. It enables you to deeply reflect on the values important to you and to fully live out the potential that you envision for yourself—and then to take small steps toward actualising the bigger picture.

HERE WE ARE COMPETENCY MATRIX

PEER RANKING		LIFE & HEALTH here to grow	HARD SKILLS here to build	GLOBAL MINDSET here to learn	PERSONAL IMPACT here to lead	SOCIAL IMPACT here to contribute	COMMUNI-CATION here to share	CREA-TIVITY here to explore
TOP 25%	VISIONARY BEST							
50 - 75%	DELIBE-RATE FOCUS							
25 - 50%	MINDFUL EXPERI-MENT							
BOTTOM 25%	SELF DISCO-VERY							

© Jannie Aasted Skov-Hansen

The seven competency dimensions are:

- **Life & Health:** Taking care of your mind and body, and tending to your wishes for a healthy and happy everyday life
- **Hard Skills:** Professional competencies
- **Global Mindset:** Capacity to function in a multicultural setting
- **Personal Impact:** Leading self and others
- **Social Impact:** Developing others
- **Communication:** Interacting with others
- **Creativity:** Curiosity, and the ability to explore opportunities.

The HERE WE ARE Competency Matrix® is based on my international experience in recruiting professionals and managers, combined with real-life examples of how fellow global professionals have unfolded and even transformed themselves during an international assignment. By becoming aware of when and how you spend your time and energy, you'll naturally focus more on the competencies you acquire. Mapping your competencies helps you plan for your next job—or simply create meaning in a global work life:

- *What's the story you'd like to tell about yourself that you will confidently bring forward in a future job interview?*
- *What are the concrete achievements, lessons and experiences that help to showcase that you possess a specific competency required for a job or organisational role?*

Jannie [author]

Competency Development Exercise

We recommend doing the following exercise after you've completed your Future Map—and each time you update your map. Allow 30 minutes for the exercise:

1. Sit together with the HERE WE ARE Competency Matrix®.
2. Find consensus with each other on which three competencies matter most for your ICC right now and in the near future (for example, when you relocate).
3. Then, individually, self-assess each of the three competencies: Where do you see yourself now, individually, compared to your peers on the competency: in the top 25%, top 50%, between 25% and 50 %, or in the bottom 25%?
4. Take turns looking at each other's ratings—and then agree on a final score on each competency for each of you individually.
5. Finally, brainstorm options for how each of you can develop further: Where do you wish to be, say, two years from now? Remember: effective development does not necessarily mean working on a weakness. Often you get more out of further developing or exploiting a strength.
6. Commit to actions and how you will support each other in realising those actions.

EXTERNAL HUMAN RESOURCES: YOUR SUPPORTERS

Human resource management entails recruiting external or temporary resources to support the ICC in achieving its objectives. Such recruitment ranges from people, such as an au pair, who support you in running the household, to members of your professional network, who support your job search.

Have another look at your ICC TimeLine. Concentrate on the 'highs'. Which person(s) were critically important in supporting and helping you through this situation as an ICC? How and where did they help you? How can you leverage such people in the future, particularly when you move to a different country?

If you conclude that you're currently missing the support you need, think about what you can do to enlist further help. Kashaf and Zaroon, during our interview, realised they lacked support in their current location, which made it difficult for both to work full-time. Following our discussion, they took action to remedy the situation. As a specific support network for ICCs, HERE WE ARE GLOBAL offers access to an ever-expanding community of people in different countries, willing to act as a local resource and help open up opportunities for professional engagement. You'll find more on this in the *Conclusion* at the end of the handbook.

Finally, add the most important elements of your network to your Future Map.

"We have help at home, and sometimes Tim's parents come over for a while. Two full-time jobs wouldn't be possible without assistance. Having a domestic helper is crucial, especially when Silje is travelling or working long hours."

Silje & Tim

"When our son was born, Joëlle and I included him in our Shared Vision. To enable both to continue working full-time, we opted for an au pair until the end of primary school. At the same time, we wanted Joseph to grow up with an identity rooted in the cultures of both parents. With Joseph growing up in a French-speaking environment (Joëlle's mother tongue), we made an effort always to recruit a Dutch-speaking au pair with an educational background. It contributed significantly to his growing up bilingual."

Paul [author]

CONTEXT

An ICC is real, not virtual. It exists in a context—of risks and opportunities—that must be taken into account so that the ICC can reach its goals. Complete your ICC Future Map with the most critical aspects of your current context: It's the starting point from which you work to achieve your strategy. Some of that context, such as the economy, is difficult to influence. Still, suppose you notice a gap between your current context and the environment you need. In that case, we recommend moving to your Secure Place to discuss how to better align your context with the desired environment.

MAPPING YOUR FUTURE AS ICC
Kashaf & Zaroon's Human Resource Management

Vision: Retirement without needing support from children
Children become global citizens

Our Secure Base
- Community of Faith
- Couple

Scenarios
- Stay abroad for next 10 years
- Zaroon progresses with current employer
- Career opportunities for Kashaf in HR for the next 5-10 years

Stakeholders
- Zaroon's employer
- Relatives back home

Our Secure Space
- Chai hour
- School & Parents

Supporters

Values and non-negotiables
- Giving back to our community

Our ICC Identity Today
- Unique in our social environment. Global Citizens connected to our Community of Faith. Anchored in Zaroon's NGO
- Professional opportunities
- School for Children

Environment that meets our needs

Key Competencies
- Development Countries
- Entrepreneur
- HR
- Finance
- Education

Context
- Post-COVID
- Developing Countries that need Education

© Paul Vanderbroeck / Jannie Aasted Skov-Hansen

Origins: South Asia; Community of Faith, different from others in home country

KEY TAKEAWAYS FROM CHAPTER 6

Congratulations, you've finished your ICC Future Map! Use it well. If an item you feel is relevant to your ICC seems to be missing, don't hesitate to add it. What matters is covering the essential elements for your ICC.

To lead the ICC to success to long-term success, its leaders need to manage its human resources. (These human resources are principally the two partners themselves.)

You can discover your couple's key competencies, as well as the environment that you need for your couple to thrive, by looking back at your history as an ICC.

Developing specific international individual competencies—for example, using the HERE WE ARE Competency Matrix®—is essential to ensuring that each partner contributes to the ICC.

To reach its goals, the ICC needs a network of external support.

ICCs exist in a context of real-world risks and opportunities. This context must be taken into account so that the ICC can reach its goals.

YOUR NOTES

CHAPTER 7

HERE WE ARE TALKING: HANDLING DAY-TO-DAY COMPLEXITY IN THE INTERNATIONAL CAREER COUPLE

The life of an ICC is complicated, isn't it? Exhausting, too. But when two talented, high-energy, dedicated people put their minds to it, they can move mountains! And that's what we see many ICCs do. They're remarkably resilient and resourceful in conducting the day-to-day business of the couple and the family. Children are brought to school, and taken care of after school; finances get paid; housing is arranged; moving companies are managed; holidays are planned; family visits are organised; and the list goes on.

Indeed, in our surveys and interviews with ICCs, they didn't mention handling daily logistics as a particular difficulty or a critical success factor. For ICCs, short-term duties and concerns, numerous as they are, don't prove to be especially daunting in and of themselves. Many ICCs are masters of multitasking. But deftly managing everyday concerns should not be a primary goal—and may impede your focus on the longer term. It's important to be aware of what is going on inside the organisation and connect it with what is going on outside (called 'integrative awareness' by Jacqueline Brassey from McKinsey).

Earlier, we showed that the research on ICCs reveals how complex they are compared with other couples. Since, you learned how to map your future, starting with your Shared Vision. Having completed your Future Map, you've arrived at the present. The time has come to focus on managing the here and now.

Below, we offer two solutions for grappling with the unique daily complexities that ICCs face, so that it all becomes less exhausting. The goal: have more time and energy to enjoy your life as an ICC—and to get your mid- and long-term aims right.

ROLE MAPPING®: WHO DOES WHAT

For any career person, it's both complicated and tiring to separate or integrate (depending on your preference) your private and professional lives. This challenge is heightened for an ICC because both partners must fulfil different roles synchronously and in parallel—and often in a foreign environment. Life in an ICC is like being in an ancient Greek play, where a single actor performed all of the various roles.

Role Mapping®, developed by Paul Vanderbroeck, is the process we propose for how partners can decide who does what, in order to optimise their private and professional responsibilities. *Role Mapping®* goes beyond figuring out how to distribute tasks at home or balance work and life. It takes into account that each partner in an ICC has many commitments that sometimes overlap and conflict. If not handled well, this reality can lead to feelings of guilt, falling short of your objectives, and tensions within the couple.

Role Mapping® empowers you to take your life in your own hands. It puts you at the helm of your commitments, rather than being driven by what's imposed on you. It lets you decide how to distribute your time and energy, how your various roles interact, and how they can reinforce one another.

We recommend doing a Role Map® once a year, or at least after each significant change—for example, after starting a new job or experiencing a relocation. If you have children, consider involving them, too. And if you have a physical Secure Space, it's a good idea to do your Role Mapping® there.

Before agreeing on who does what in your couple, you first must gain insight about the various roles each of you plays and how they interrelate. The mapping process helps you identify sources of tension and opportunities for improvement.

"We take joint responsibility for parenting and the household: a 50/50 split. However, we also support the partner who is undergoing a professional change, or who has a lot to do for a while at work, or who has more work-related travel. That support might, for example, involve taking on more of the domestic tasks. We create space for each other and seek to realise the full potential in each other's lives."

Silje & Tim

ROLE MAPPING® EXERCISE

Role Mapping® is best done manually. You need these items: at least four large sheets of paper (flipchart paper is the most useful), markers, and a stack of sticky notes in different sizes, forms and three different colours. Allow 90 minutes for this exercise.

1. As individuals (not together), prepare a Role Map® of the different roles you currently have at work and outside of work. Here are some basic principles and features of the Role Map®:
   a. This first iteration of the map should depict the present situation: how your roles currently rank in importance — and how they interact with one another in constructive and not so constructive ways.
   b. A Role Map® captures what's really going on in your professional and personal life.
   c. The most informative Role Maps® vary the shapes of objects (the size of sticky notes) to show how roles differ in weight (how much time and energy they take up).
   d. By using different-colour sticky notes, you represent which parts of your life the roles touch: one colour for professional roles (such as 'Manager', 'Financial Controller'), a second colour for private-life roles ('parent', 'spouse'), and a third colour for other non-professioal roles ('treasurer of the parents' association', 'goalkeeper of the handball team').
   e. You can also draw lines and arrows (or other symbols) to show how the roles interrelate and reinforce one another, or where there's tension between roles.

Example of the Role Map® of a partner in an ICC

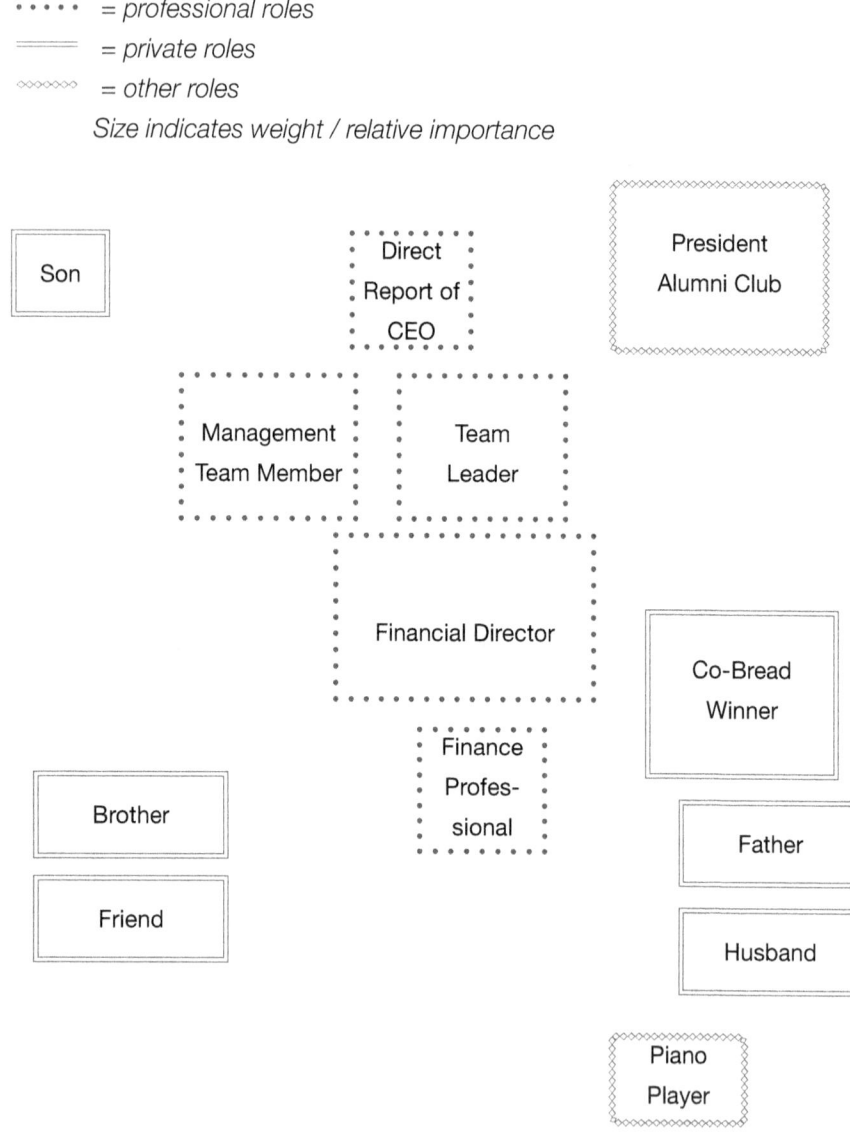

2. In your couple, analyse the two Role Maps® one after the other.
   a. Partner A presents his or her Role Map® to Partner B.
   b. Partner B asks clarifying questions where needed and, most important, gives feedback on the Role Map®.
   c. Together, identify one or two opportunities for optimisation or reducing tension between or among roles.
   d. Review the assessment of your Key ICC Competencies and International Competencies (Chapter 6 – Here We Are Developing). Look for possibilities to optimise the distribution of roles within your ICC by leveraging each partner's strengths.
   e. Do the same for the Role Map® of Partner B.
3. Next, work again individually: modify your Role Map® — for example, by moving and changing the sticky notes — according to the improvements you've identified. The goal: end up with a Role Map® that contains less tension and whose various roles reinforce rather than weaken one another.
4. Come back together to present and discuss the future Role Map®.
   a. Then agree what actions you must take to realise the changes you seek.
   b. In the end, agree when you will sit together again to discuss progress on the changes.

> *"In Europe, Martin worked, and I studied and took care of the kids. Martin was very busy but still available for the kids. I was not in favour of Martin's working so much, but I supported him all the way. It's the result of our underlying values: honesty, trust and endless talk. Each of us added something unique."*
>
> John

TALKING MEANS DIALOGUE

"We need to talk" is often an anxiety-provoking statement, signalling that something important has occurred and that you didn't notice it. To anticipate and prepare for such moments, ICCs need to have regular conversations about how things are going and what the future looks like.

The ICCs we interviewed emphasized the importance of talk—lots of it—in their couple. It's difficult to talk through difficult situations, involving interests or viewpoints that conflict or whose stakes are high, particularly for people who love each other. Agreeing on a Shared Vision and Mutual Career Support requires high-level communication skills. It's what's supposed to happen in the Secure Space.

As we keep emphasising, the ICC is both an organisation *and* a couple. The partners' love results in a higher level of tolerance than in a work organisation—but it also makes communication more challenging, as Zaroon expresses:

> "You don't feel comfortable when you're progressing and your wife isn't. Sometimes I hesitate to share my successes with Kashaf.
>
> Zaroon

Effective discussion techniques are found in organisational theory and in couples therapy. Indeed, the field of organisational development has adopted best practices from couples therapy in teaching work colleagues how to reach agreement through dialogue. If your assessment of Key ICC Competencies and International Competencies (*Chapter 6 — Here we are developing*) identifies a need in this area, we suggest consulting one or more of the many helpful books, articles and videos about effective communication that you can find online or in shops. The titles and search terms often refer to 'difficult', 'courageous' or 'crucial' conversations.

We suggest that ICCs create time and space for such

discussions on a regular basis. There's no need for a weekly strategy meeting on a big topic. Just be together and be mindful that these talks operate on a different level than when you're figuring out who goes to the next parents' meeting. That's because these conversations help you assess whether you're on track with your ICC strategy, according to plan, and whether any change is on the horizon. It's your chance to share essential information and impressions—and to get support from each other, both emotionally and practically.

Regarding mutual support, shared leadership within the ICC does not mean having two people always in the lead simultaneously. It often involves switching the leader and follower roles back-and-forth. In this dynamic, 'tough empathy' is a helpful concept from London Business School professors Rob Goffee and Gareth Jones. Tough empathy means actively caring about, and empathising strongly with, the follower. At the same time, a leader doesn't necessarily give the follower what he or she wants, but rather what the person needs for his or her success. Tough empathy is similar to care to dare, which we introduced earlier for Mutual Career Development. It therefore is an effective style for both development and motivation.

> "Building the healthcare company was a challenge. We bought the property spontaneously. It was a big investment. I intuitively knew there was a market. Yet we only went ahead after Martin managed to impose that we do a solid business plan."
>
> John

'Conversation' does not accurately describe how ICCs should discuss crucial matters. 'Dialogue' is a better word. Our aim is neither to be pedantic nor to get mired in semantics. We merely want to clarify what substantive communication in an ICC really involves.

In its Latin etymology, 'conversation' means 'turning things around'. Sure, that covers some of what should happen so that partners look at a matter from different perspectives, increase mutual understanding, and reach a better decision. But that's not all of it.

Dialogue, to hark back to the ancient Greek, is what happens through (*dia*) debate and reasoning (*logos*). Dialogue reaches an outcome not just through an exchange of ideas, facts and perspectives (that's 'conversation'); it's also a thought process, both individual and collective.

Of course, day-to-day discussions within a couple need not always involve dialogue. But matters of importance to the ICC certainly should.

"I recently coached a Director in the UN for a period of 12 months. During that time, he was promoted to a very senior regional position based in South Asia. He moved there with their young child. It was a great job, but a hardship posting. His wife, who had a senior job with another humanitarian organisation, was at first expected to stay behind for a maximum of one year. The plan was that she should be able to arrange a transfer or land an equivalent job locally. It was a stressful and challenging period for him. I'm glad my coaching helped him to overcome the separation and to motivate his wife to stay the course to work out a good solution. Before the year was over, she made it to his host country in a job that worked for her."

Paul [author]

Regarding techniques for dialogue, we can add little that's particular to ICCs rather than couples in general. We also hesitate to prescribe a particular way of interacting for a process that is—and should be—unique to each couple. Let's merely emphasise the key principles of successful dialogue:
- A clear agenda for the dialogue creates focus and avoids talking at cross purposes.
- Dialogue requires an environment where both partners feel safe, such as a Secure Space.

- Facts and feelings come first. Judgement comes later.
- Active listening (open questions, probing, checking understanding) from both partners gets all facts and feelings on the table.
- It's helpful to make an effort to understand your partner while looking for both spoken and unspoken cues and messages.
- The Western world often overestimates the importance of words in communication, and underemphasises intonation and body langue. The Japanese appropriately refer to 'reading the air' in describing how people detect and understand unspoken messages. This principle is key to any dialogue, but especially if the two partners grew up in different cultures. Gender differences also can play a role in opposite-sex couples.
- It's fundamental to (proactively) share feelings, both about the item on the agenda and about how the dialogue is proceeding in real time.
- When you have strong feelings, the famous 'counting to ten' before speaking does help. Taking a breath allows you to calm down and still express yourself, but in a way that helps your counterpart understand and empathise. Sometimes it also gives you the time to reflect so that you can combine expressing your feelings with a constructive proposal. And if you're a person who bubbles over with enthusiasm when you have a brilliant idea, taking a breather gives your partner time to process what you're trying to convey without being overwhelmed by your stream of words and, perhaps, gesticulations. Taking a breath is especially helpful when the two partners have grown up in different cultures.

We conclude this chapter with a powerful quotation from one of the ICCs who accompanied us throughout this handbook.

"The foundation of our couple is so solid that we never need to question any aspect of the relationship. It allows both of us to direct our energy elsewhere—namely, to our respective passions. We never doubt the relationship, even during a fight. Wherever we fight, we fight within the container of good. Mind you, it's bloody hard to make it work."

John & Martin

KEY TAKEAWAYS FROM CHAPTER 7

The high level of complexity faced by ICCs poses particular challenges in their daily lives.

Life for ICCs becomes less complex if they communicate well and if they know how to distribute their various roles inside and outside the ICC.

Role Mapping® empowers you to decide how to allocate your time and energy, how your various roles interact, and how they can reinforce one another.

Talking, or rather dialogue, within the ICC is key to decision-making and reaching agreements.

Dialogue means debating about ideas, feelings and facts—and engaging in both an individual and a collective thought process. It is not mere 'conversation'.

ICCs can benefit from communication techniques that have been developed for organisations and couples therapy.

YOUR NOTES

CONCLUSION

HERE WE STOP

We've come to the end of our story. If you've arrived here after reading the previous chapters and completing its exercises, then you have mapped your future as an ICC and agreed on actions to get you there. Further support can assist you in implementing those actions, executing your current and future moves, and conducting your daily business as an ICC.

HERE WE ARE GLOBAL has created a website, a network and partnerships focusing on the international mobility of couples and families. You can get access to specific resources, services and people — depending on your needs. Some features are available free of charge; others require a fee. Volunteers run the local chapter activities on personal and professional development. They offer a real opportunity for any travelling partner in an ICC to jumpstart a professional life in a new country.

You also can access the HERE WE ARE Academy through the website. It has plenty of learning activities, and you can ses we've proposed in this book. You can also book coaching sessions for your ICC.

Check it out, and sign up for the newsletter!

www.herewareglobal.com

So, here we are! We hope you have enjoyed reading this book as much as we have enjoyed bringing it to life. Even after publication, we continue to develop and refine the community, activities and services around personal and professional development through HERE WE ARE GLOBAL. We invite you to stay connected!

We routinely team up with others who are keen to write a new narrative on dual global careers. This teamwork allows us all to unfold our potential and create meaning—no matter where we are in the world.

When working virtually in global teams, we often end our meetings with a round of 'check out'. Each participant leaves after briefly sharing what he or she is inspired to say as a concluding comment. So—check out from you, Paul?

"So glad to have been able to bring together ideas and experiences that I've built up over the years for the benefit of a group of people whose passions and challenges I empathise with."

Paul [author]

And from you, Jannie?

"Grateful for this opportunity to be a magnifying glass for so many wholehearted and talented fellow global explorers!"

Jannie [author]

Thanks for staying with us this far. We wish you lots of success and happiness in your professional and personal life as an International Career Couple. Do let us know how the book has helped you. We are here to learn!

BIBLIOGRAPHY
– HERE'S WHAT WE'VE READ

Adam, H., Obodaru, O., Lu, J.G., Maddux, W.W., Galinsky, A.D. 2018, The shortest path to oneself leads around the world: Living abroad increases self-concept clarity, *Organizational Behavior and Human Decision Processes*, Volume 145, 2018, 16-29.

Bathmann, N., Cornelißen, W., Müller, D. 2013, *Gemeinsam zum Erfolg? Berufliche Karrieren von Frauen in Paarbeziehungen*, Wiesbaden: Springer VS.

Block, P. 2016, *The Empowered Manager: Positive Political Skills at Work*, Hoboken: Whiley.

Brassey, J., Kruyt, M. 2020, How to demonstrate calm and optimism in a crisis, *McKinsey & Company*, https://mck.co/2YrP2sm

Campbell, D. 1990, *If You Don't Know Where You're Going, You'll Probably End Up Somewhere Else*, Allen: Thomas More Association.

Carnot, A. 2016, *Chéri(e) on s'expatrie! Guide de survie à l'usage des couples aventuriers*, Paris : Eyrolles.

Ferrante, M.B. 2019, McKinsey's Innovative Dual Career Program Focuses On Families Where Both Parents Work, *Forbes.com* Jan 31, accessed 29/05/2019.

Goffee, R., Jones, G. 2000, Why should anyone be led by you?, *Harvard Business Review*, 78(5), 62–70.

Kohlrieser, G., Goldsworthy, S., Coombe, D. 2012, *Care to Dare: Unleashing Astonishing Potential Through Secure Base Leadership,* San Francisco: Jossey-Bass

Internations 2018, *Expat Insider Business Edition Country Focus*, https://bit.ly/2Wk3VOc.

Känsälä, M., Mäkelä, L, Suutari, V. 2015, Career coordination strategies among dual career expatriate couples, *The International Journal of Human Resource Management,* Vol. 26, No. 17, 2187–2210.

Kierner, A. 2018, Expatriated dual-career partners: Hope and disillusionment, *Journal of Global Mobility*, Vol. 6 No. 3/4, 244-257.

Kotter, J.P. 1995, Leading Change. Why Transformation Efforts Fail, *Harvard Business Review,* March-April, 3-10.

Linehan, M., Scullion, H., Mattl, C. 2005, Topmanagerinnen und Dual-Career Couples auf Auslandsentsendung, in: Stahl, G. K., Mayrhofer, W., Kühlmann, T. M. (eds), *Internationales Personalmanagement. Neue Aufgaben, neue Lösungen*, München: Rainer Hampp, 347-362.

Mäkelä, L, Känsälä, M., Suutari, V. 2011, The roles of expatriates' spouses among dual career couples, *Cross Cultural Management: An International Journal*, Vol. 18 Issue: 2, 185-197.

McFarland, W., Goldsworthy, S. 2014, *Choosing Change. How Leaders and Organizations Drive Results One Person at a Time*, New York: McGraw Hill.

McKinsey & Company, LeanIn 2017, *Women in the Workplace.*

McNulty, Y. 2012, "Being dumped in to sink or swim': an empirical study of organizational support for the trailing spouse", *Human Resource Development International*, Vol. 15 No. 4, 417-434.

McNulty, Y. 2015, Till stress do us part: the causes and consequences of expatriate divorce, *Journal of Global Mobility,* Vol. 3 no. 2, 106-136.

McNulty, Y., Moeller M. 2018, 'A typology of dual-career expatriate (trailing) spouses: The 'R' profile', In Dickmann, M., Suutari, V., Wurtz, O. (eds.), *The Management of Global Careers: Exploring the Rise of International Work*, London, Palgrave-Macmillan, pp 257-290.

Netexpat, EY 2018, Relocating Partner Survey Report, https://go.ey.com/2TolB4u.

Permits Foundation, 2012, *International Mobility and Dual Career Survey of International Employees*, https://bit.ly/3abjPOL.

Petriglieri, G., Petriglieri, J.L., Wood, J. 2018, Fast Tracks and Inner Journeys: Crafting Portable Selves for Contemporary Careers, *Administrative Science Quarterly*, Vol. 63 (3), 479-525.

Petriglieri, J. 2018, Talent Management and the Dual Career Couple, *Harvard Business Review*. May/Jun, Vol. 96 Issue 3, pp. 106-113.

Petriglieri, J. 2019, *Couples That Work: How Dual-Career Couples Can Thrive in Love and Work*, Cambridge: Harvard UP.

Petriglieri, J., Obodaru, O. 2019, Secure-base Relationships as Drivers of Professional Identity Development in Dual-career Couples, *Administrative Science Quarterly*, vol. 64, no. 3, pp. 694-736.

Ramarajan, L., Reid, E. 2013. Shattering the Myth of Separate Worlds: Negotiating Nonwork Identities at Work. *Academy of Management Review*, Vol. 38, No. 4, 621–644.

Santa Fe Relocation 2019, *The Global Mobility Survey 2019*, https://bit.ly/3fzpRtu.

Schreyögg, A. 2013, *Familie trotz Doppelkarriere. Vom Dual Career zum Dual Care Couple*, Wiesbaden: Springer VS.

Shortland, S. 2020, Career cooperation, coordination, compatibility and co-working: How female expatriates mobilise dual-career strategies, *Gender in Management*, Vol. 35 No. 2, pp. 121-139.

Thompson, D. 2020, When a Promotion Leads to Divorce, *the Atlantic,* January 14. https://bit.ly/2WzsYe5.

Wilson, R.F. 2008, Keeping women in business (and family), in: Gregg S, Stoner, J.R., *Rethinking Business Management. Examining the Foundations of Business Education*, Distributed Presses, 2008.

Wittenberg-Cox, A. 2018, Being a Two-Career Couple Requires a Long-Term Plan, *hbr.org,* February 26.

SO, HERE WE ARE, ABOUT THE AUTHORS

Paul Vanderbroeck
Leadership Coach
& Career Consultant

- 15 years HR in multinationals
- Executive Coach and Career Consultant
- 2x Expatriate / 2x Self-mover / 1x Travelling Partner
- Visiting Professor at Business Schools
- Passionate about Developing Potential
- Author of Leadership Strategies for Women
- Co-Author of HERE WE ARE The ICC Handbook
- PhD in History and Sociology
- Partner in International Career Couple
- Dutch and Swiss nationalilty
- Father of two

Jannie Aasted Skov-Hansen Skov-Hansen

Senior HR Consultant
& Founder of HERE WE ARE GLOBAL

- 12 years HR /Global Mobility
- 7 years Travelling Partner in Nepal and Kyrgyzstan
- Change Management Professional
- Founder of HERE WE ARE GLOBAL
- Partner in International Career Couple
- MA in Danish language and Organisational Psychology
- What could be next?
- Co-Author of *HERE WE ARE The ICC Handbook*
- Danish and mother of three
- Chair of Governing Board at an IB school
- Global Leadership Coach

www.ingramcontent.com/pod-product-compliance
Lightning Source LLC
Chambersburg PA
CBHW071731080526
44588CB00013B/1988